T0208586

How to Fulfill Your Purpose

JAMES CULVER BRYANT

BALBOA.
PRESS
A DIVISION OF HAY HOUSE

Balboa Press books may be ordered through booksellers or by contacting:

Balboa Press
A Division of Hay House
1663 Liberty Drive
Bloomington, IN 47403
www.balboapress.com
1 (877) 407-4847

Print information available on the last page.

ISBN: 978-1-9822-3522-2 (sc)
ISBN: 978-1-9822-3523-9 (e)

Balboa Press rev. date: 10/02/2019

CONTENTS

Introduction vii

Chapter 1   Evolution 1
Chapter 2   Preparation 24
Chapter 3   Prepare Yourself 32
Chapter 4   Healing Your Body 41
Chapter 5   Your Conscious Mind 52
Chapter 6   Your Unconscious Mind 61
Chapter 7   Healing Your Spirit 67
Chapter 8   Attachments 75
Chapter 9   Spirit Realm 84
Chapter 10 The New You 91

INTRODUCTION

Our lives have a purpose. The purpose is to consciously experience the events that arise in the course of our lives. It's said that nothing happens by accident. This is true. There is a reason for each experience we encounter. We don't know the reasons. Life would be much easier if we did. All we can do is to follow our hearts' desire, notice what we notice, show up, and do our best.

Achieving your purpose is predicated on your ability to have the courage to engage in the experiences that show up. That's your purpose—*live the experience.*

Fortunately, there is a plan—a blueprint. We come into life with an imprinted plan designed to offer us all of the experiences needed for the work of this life. I suggest you Google "soul imprint" or "soul blueprint" to learn more. The imprinting resides in our unconscious, which is the source of our heart's desire. The reason we notice something, or someone, in the first place is because we are supposed to experience something. We may need to experience a relationship with someone or have a career that offers us the experience needed for a future challenge. Notice I haven't mentioned *knowing* or *understanding* as our life's purpose. Knowing and understanding are not required. It's the *experience* that's required.

When we decide to fulfill our purpose, we are deciding to evolve from an ego-centered to a soul-centered life. I think of the ego as having a fear-based orientation. The ego is supposed to keep us safe, know what to do, and be in control. The soul is free from debilitating fear. Our soul knows it's safe, doesn't need to be in control, and is our divinity within.

I'm sharing my experiences as an example of how to move from an ego-centered to a soul-centered life. It's a story that's intended to provide all you will need to make your life a spiritual journey. A spiritual journey is simply a life that's lived with the intention to fulfill your purpose. It's a life that's soul-directed instead of being mind-directed. When your soul points the way, all you have to do is to show up and do your best. As you might imagine, the shift from a mind-centered to a soul-centered life requires creating a new normal.

The first task in creating a new normal is to become aware of your current normal. It's hard to be aware of what has always been your normal. It takes some kind of experience that causes you to recognize a pattern or behavior that has been automatic. The experience doesn't have to be anything other than a wakeup call. One such experience happened to me during a horseback ride.

I'd never been on a horse before. I had watched a lot of cowboy movies, which made riding look easy. I climbed up on my horse and said the magic words. Just like in the movies, the horse started to walk down the path. I thought I was in control, but I wasn't. About thirty minutes into the ride, the horse took the bit in its teeth and started toward the barn. No matter how much I tugged on the reins, the horse didn't flinch from its intended path back to the barn.

Life is like a horseback ride, and I'm the horse. I have a rider that I mostly ignore because I know where I want to go. I want to stay on the familiar path and return to the barn. This is my normal, and that's just the way it is—and always has been and always will be. I don't realize how hard my soul is tugging on the reins to get me to go where it wants me to go—to experience what it wants me to experience.

I have to take the bit out of my teeth if I'm going to create a new normal. This is an act of self-sacrifice necessary to become free from my mind's agenda. I have to sacrifice my thinking mind. I have to walk in the moment-by-moment experience of the ride, noticing the slightest movement of the reins. My mind is too limited to know what's best for me. However, I will continue to take my mind along on the ride so I will be able to participate—enjoy what's around the next bend. Thus my purpose is to carry my soul through life as it guides me from one experience to the next.

Now that I'm an old horse, I can look back in retrospect and recognize how my life fits together. I'm amazed at how experiences unfolded in just the right order to prepare me for what was next. There was no way to prepare for what was coming. All I could do was show up and do my best.

The chapters that follow chronicle my journey to fulfill my purpose as it teaches you how to fulfill your purpose. The process begins with becoming conscious. You must develop your internal witness who listens to what you are saying and allows you to become aware of awareness—aware of your automatic thinking and everything you take for granted. Without awareness, you don't recognize that you are living the same day over and over. You will not recognize that your mind is keeping you from achieving your purpose.

Chapter 1 is about evolution. The mechanism of evolution is through our experience. Life experiences set us up and prepare us for this change. I use my experiences to illustrate how I evolved from being an unconscious adolescent to becoming an adult who was aware there was a lot more to life than I thought. I learned that following my intuition was the only way to fulfill my purpose.

We are given the means to tap into our ability to be inspired, whether inspiration comes as a thought out of the blue or through intuition. How inspiration comes to us doesn't matter as much as noticing it and being able to follow through.

You will be introduced to synchronicity and how it serves to provide solutions and opportunities to create your new normal.

Chapters 2 and 3 are about how we are being prepared throughout our life to accomplish the challenges that arise. It includes an account by a Pentagon official who showed up and went into action on the morning of September 11, 2001. Her story contains elements of how preparation, synchronicity, and intuition combined to provide everything she needed to meet the challenge.

You must have enough psychological freedom to make decisions, and this chapter addresses how past events that produced limiting beliefs must be resolved. One section describes managing your thinking and focusing awareness. Tips on developing your awareness and trusting your intuition are also included.

Chapter 4 deals with healing your body from the effects of traumatic memories, with accounts of how others have resolved symptoms associated with body memories. Your body stores past trauma and automatically reacts to situations that trigger old wounds. You will learn about somatic pain and how to heal from emotional wounds.

Healing from these wounds is an essential part of your transition from being held hostage to the past to being free from your history. The goal is to be free from what's holding you back from your potential.

Chapters 5 and 6 address your conscious and unconscious mind, as well as the impact of heredity and your history. Taking charge of automatic thinking, and recognizing how your past is influencing your present, are part of becoming free enough to create your new normal.

Chapter 7 is about preparing for the transition from your current normal to turning your life into a journey, free from beliefs and fears that hold you hostage.

As in any transition, you must let go of your old normal and travel through the confusion of change to create your new normal—a spirit having a life experience. As with any voyage into the unknown, you start by making all the preparations for getting underway. In this case, you are preparing your mind, body, and spirit for a new normal, which will allow you to succeed in fulfilling your purpose.

As a spirit having a life experience, you will learn how the journey you have made through many lives, including this one, may have resulted in your spirit energy being split away from your soul. This chapter will teach you how to bring your spirit energy back into wholeness with your soul.

Many examples show how others were able to bring home their fragmented spirit energy. One story includes how spirits helped me help my client restore a fragmented personality. When a personality splits up to survive a traumatic event, it takes its spirit energy with it. Healing is necessary to become whole again.

You are never alone throughout your journey. Having the help of a spirit who talked to me through the client taught me I was not alone—not in my healing work and not in my own life. Neither are you.

Chapter 8 takes you beyond your mind and into the world of spirit energy. Everything is energy. Energy can be neither created nor destroyed, but it can be split up into segments or parts. There are stories of how people were able to take their spirit energy back from others and how they sent away the spirit energy of others.

Chapter 9 addresses fragmentation of spirit energy and

resolving past life trauma that is influencing this life. There are stories of how a past life event can affect relationships.

Chapter 10 invites you to create your new normal and provides information about how having a new normal might affect relationships with your old friends. You will learn how surrendering your old normal is part of creating your new normal. Of course, there isn't a "normal" because we are evolving all the time. I have discovered that change is the only normal.

Creating a new normal requires noticing your automatic thinking and thinking about your beliefs. You may not change any of your beliefs, but you will have a chance to think about them.

It's difficult to become aware of what has always been. We all think of things as being just the way they are—until something happens to cause us to take notice.

In 1961, I moved from Redwood City, California, where I had grown up, to Pensacola, Florida, where I started training in the Naval Air Basic Training Command. I was used to a life in California that was a lot different from life in Florida. In Florida, segregation was the norm. I had never even thought about having to drink from a "Whites Only" drinking fountain or avoid sitting in the back of the bus. Schools in Florida were segregated, as were public swimming pools. I remember sitting at poolside on the navy base when a black man jumped into the pool. Several white people jumped out. That was just how life was in Florida. It was what it was. Only becoming aware created a new normal. We humans tend to accept situations that have been within our normal experience until something happens to cause us to take notice, stop, and think. We are not even aware of our normal until something causes us to stop and think—to become aware, to become conscious.

CHAPTER 1

Evolution

My Early Experiences

The mechanism of evolution is having an experience. Life experiences set us up and prepare us for the next challenge. What I have noticed in my own life is that the more resistant I am to change, the more extreme is the experience needed for me to evolve. At nineteen, for example, I was happy working at a gas station. Yes, pumping gas in a winter rain was uncomfortable. Yet life was good. I had no interest in changing. I wasn't motivated to do anything other than what I was doing. I had obtained a two-year college degree and was taking flying lessons at the local airport and hanging out with a friend who had his own plane. It's a wonder we didn't kill ourselves.

I began dating the counter waitress at the drugstore across the street from the gas station where I worked. Back in those days, a guy had to look good, so I drove a Corvette. I had it all: money, a girlfriend, a fast car, and a job in a gas station. I was invincible. My ego was having a great time.

What is ego? I think of it as a perpetual teenager who avoids pain and seeks pleasure. All egos run on a fear-based operating system that places winning ahead of losing. Ego thinks it must always win.

Unfortunately, neither of these goals is obtainable. So there I was, an ego with no plan. As I look back, I can see that having no plan was just what was best for me. There was no plan to get in the way of what was to happen next.

Vietnam happened next. My resistance to change dissolved with the fear of being drafted into the army. I had just graduated from San Mateo Junior College in California when I received a letter from the draft board telling me I was now classified 1A. I could be drafted any day. Fear was the feeling. Action was the result.

I thought it would be a great idea to have the military teach me how to fly. If I were a pilot, I wouldn't be slogging through a Vietnamese jungle, wet and miserable. I drove to the San Mateo County courthouse to join the air force. The recruiter met me with a smile and asked me if I had a four-year college degree. I told him I had an associate of arts degree. He said I didn't meet the minimum educational requirements. I found the army recruiter, who met me with a smile. I asked if I could get into their flight training program. I received the same question regarding my education and the same answer—not qualified.

As I stepped out of the army recruiting office, a navy chief petty officer motioned me over with a smile and asked how tall I was.

"About five-seven," I said.

He told me about the Naval Aviation Cadet Program (NAVCAD). If I could pass the physical exam and all of the entrance tests, plus complete flight training, I would be a naval aviator and commissioned as an ensign. I signed up.

At twenty-one, I didn't know what I was doing or what I was getting into. I sold my Corvette because the monthly payments were more than my NAVCAD pay and flew from San Francisco to Pensacola, Florida, to start my military career.

This snippet of my life story contains everything I needed to know about life, but I couldn't see it at the time. In retrospect, I can see that I really didn't have a plan other than doing what I liked doing—flying. I had no master plan. Yet, there was a master plan. I carried an internal blueprint I was unknowingly following.

Looking back, I noticed that I had left my home in Redwood City, California, and moved to Pensacola, Florida, because my future was going to unfold elsewhere. Events were redirecting my life. My internal blueprint was guiding me from one experience to the next. I was having every experience I needed to prepare me to give up my ego and serve the very God I believed didn't care about me. After all, He couldn't care much because my mother died suddenly when I was nineteen.

Since I was a know-it-all, it took some extreme events to overcome my resistance. And I was now in the perfect place for extreme experiences. As a naval aviator, I was flying off and on aircraft carriers, using my aviator ego to keep me alive. Little did I know I was being kept alive for a reason, and my inflated ego had little to do with my survival.

At this time of my life, my only heart's desire was to fly airplanes. I didn't know what my purpose was. Since I didn't know my purpose, I thought I'd just do what I enjoyed doing. That didn't mean I'd sit back and wait for food to be brought to me. If I had, I would have starved to death a long time ago. Life is hard for a reason.

Adversity strengthens us, builds our tolerance, and prepares us to take on greater challenges. Each experience provides us something. No experience is wasted. We only learn in retrospect what that something is. One sunny day I learned something about myself I would have never learned unless something bad happened—or at least I thought it was bad at the time.

My copilot and I had launched from the aircraft carrier to perform some post-maintenance checks of the aircraft. About an hour into our flight, I felt the aircraft shudder. I checked my instruments and noticed that the number-two-engine power indicator was showing a loss of power. I asked my copilot to check the right engine.

He turned in his seat to look at the engine and gasped. "We're streaming smoke!"

Training took over. My right hand automatically moved where it need to go. I feathered the engine, and we stopped streaming smoke.

I asked the captain of my aircraft carrier if I could land aboard the ship. I had to let the ship know I had lost an engine and wanted to land as soon as I returned to the ship. This meant the ship would have to stop preparations for the next launch to get the deck ready for my unscheduled arrival. The ship's captain granted permission, and I proceeded to make a safe landing. Without the engine failure, I would have never had the opportunity to discover how well I could make a single-engine landing aboard ship. A bad situation turned into a good one. At the time, I couldn't have known how things would turn out. This is where trust comes in.

I wouldn't have had the idea to land aboard ship if I wasn't supposed to have the positive experience that I needed. If I had crashed on deck, it would have been another kind of experience! No experience is wasted.

I must have needed another experience that taught me to trust my instincts. I was a pragmatic carrier pilot and one of the catapult officers on the USS *Independence* (CVA-62). Catapult officers are responsible for the safe launch of aircraft from the aircraft carrier. They are trained in the operation and maintenance of the catapult and serve as the division officers for the catapult crew. The cat crew is busy both on the flight deck and below deck, operating the massive machinery necessary to move a fifty thousand–pound aircraft from 0 to 130 miles an hour in about 180 feet. Cat officers are like orchestra conductors. They must be situationally aware of everything. They perform a prelaunch inspection of the catapult and ensure all the necessary equipment is in place before launch. During the launching evolution, the cat officer directs the cat crew in connecting the aircraft to the catapult and signals the pilot to power up for launch. Once the pilot signals he or she is ready to launch, the cat officer makes a final scan of the area to ensure everything is safe for launch and then touches the flight deck, which is the signal to launch the aircraft.

What happened during a normal launch will stay with me for the rest of my life. I was about to launch an F-4 Phantom fighter jet when I suddenly stopped. I was about to touch the deck to give the launch signal to accelerate the fighter from zero to well over one hundred miles an hour. The F-4 was in afterburner. The pilot had saluted, signaling he was ready to be launched, and I had a clear deck to go ahead and give the launch signal. But something came over me.

I froze within inches of completing the launch signal. I stayed frozen in place, not knowing why. Then I saw a RA-5C Vigilante, the largest aircraft on the carrier, taxiing up the flight deck alongside the F-4 Phantom on the catapult. Still frozen, I watched as the taxi director turned the RA-5C so its tail was right in front of the fighter on the catapult. The pilot's eyes were wide open as he expected to die in the next moment. I suspended the launch, and we all looked at each other.

If I had given the launch signal, the F-4 would have collided with the tail of the RA-5C, causing a massive explosion. The fact that an aircraft was taxiing up the flight deck alongside the catapult was not out of the ordinary. The problem occurred when the taxi director turned the plane in a way as to cause its tail to cross in front of the F-4 that was about to be launched. This accident was about to happen, and I seemed to know it was coming.

The next day I was having breakfast in the dirty-shirt wardroom. Along with the ship's formal wardroom where officers have to be dressed in the uniform of the day and are served their food, there is a cafeteria-style, dirty-shirt wardroom where pilots can eat in their flight suits, and officers who work on the flight deck do not have to change into the uniform of the day. I was having my breakfast before going topside when I felt the presence of a big guy standing next to me. (Remember, I'm five-foot-seven.) His flight suit gave him away as being a pilot. He asked me if I was the cat officer yesterday morning. I said I was, and he thanked me for saving his life.

I jokingly said, "I was saving mine. And you're welcome."

This experience taught me to always follow my instincts. I believe it was an example of my instincts pushing through and stopping me in my tracks. I was definitely getting information from a source other than my mind. It was a life-changing event. Along with several other events, it caused my old normal to come unglued and a new normal to start forming. By the end of the cruise, I had learned that something bigger than my ego was keeping me alive.

My experiences where propelling me (no aviation pun intended) along my journey—fulfilling my purpose.

The final experience that destroyed my idea of myself came on the last day of a six-month cruise. The air wing of fifty aircraft had flown off the ship the day before, leaving a single F-4 to be launched the next morning. I was standing on four empty acres of flight deck with only one aircraft to launch. During a normal launch, I would be launching from two catapults as fast I could. Today should have been easy.

The deck was wet with dew as the F-4 taxied toward the catapult. It had no weapons and minimum fuel, which made it much lighter than normal. Usually an F-4 needs its afterburners to take off, but not this morning. The pilot went to full power and saluted. He was ready to be launched. I gave the launch signal, and the F-4 started down the catapult track, rotated, and flew off.

As the aircraft rotated, up came an eight-by-ten-inch steel plate that had been hit by the jet blast. The steel plate started down the flight deck right at me. I watched it slip and slide on the wet deck, slowly coming toward me. It traveled about 180 feet and stopped right between my feet. I bent over, picked it up, and handed it to the catapult captain. Then I looked up and gave thanks that the F-4 was not in afterburner. If it was, I probably would have been killed.

The event woke me up. I went from being an agnostic to believing that a presence was guiding and protecting me. I believe this was the moment when I began to believe there is a larger plan and a journey to be taken. I woke up and recognized there was more to life than I could ever have imagined.

I was being kept alive to fulfill a purpose. There were just too many times I could have died. Somehow, I knew I wasn't alone. Up until this point in my life, I had assumed I was alone. Life was up to me to figure out and find success. My experiences during this cruise as a catapult officer taught me that I am a player on a universal team and that life is a journey to be experienced.

Evolving the Ego

We are all on a journey, and knowing that changes how we experience life. In my case, I believe I started to wake up with my experience in the navy and become more conscious of what was going on in my life. I began to be aware of my automatic thinking, becoming conscious of my need to be flexible, holding loosely what I thought I knew. After all, knowledge is just a placeholder until new knowledge comes along.

Many years later, I realized that even though I had come to believe in divine guidance, I still had an ego that needed to evolve. When I retired after twenty-six years in the navy, I was dealing with a failed marriage and a career change. I had been running from one identity to another. I didn't know what to do.

An old saying in aviation goes, "Never get out of altitude, airspeed, and ideas at the same time." I was participating in a guided imagery exercise as part of a transition workshop when I imagined my exhausted ego clinging onto a cliff by its fingernails. I was afraid to let go for the fear of what might happen. Suddenly, I found myself in midair and about to fall. My fingers must have run out of the strength needed to cling to the rocks of the cliff. I started to fall. Yet I didn't fall more than an inch when I experienced being caught by a force much stronger than I was. Whatever caught me seemed to be waiting to catch me, just waiting for my ego to surrender and let go. That experience was a turning point along my journey. It changed my old belief that life was all up to me, to become a person having a life experience. My mind and its ego still had to do everything, but they were not expected to know what to do. What to do came to me from another source—my unconscious blueprint.

Well, I asked myself, *now what do I do? If my ego isn't going to run my life, what is?* Here is where the evolution from who I thought I was to who I would become started. When my ego surrendered, I stopped having to prove anything. I didn't have to hang my hat on being a navy commander or a carrier pilot. Having been both, I knew neither one was who I really was.

To create a new normal, I had to move past the need to subscribe to a social or political ideology. I recognized that any such identity is limiting, putting one in a box filled with all the expectations that ideology or identity entails. Now that I was free from any identity attachments, what was going to happen to fill the void? I pondered this question for a long time before giving up. I finally realized that all I had to do was follow my intuition and let the outcomes unfold. It took decades before realizing my soul was the source of my intuition. I didn't know I always had everything I needed within me.

"Let go and let God," is an expression in the twelve-step program. Letting go is realizing your ego does not have the ability to choose the path that will give you the experiences you need. The irony is that God is within you, so the expression should be, "Let go and allow your blueprint to be experienced." I believed that my intuition was the guide, but I was really getting directions from my soul. Either way, it doesn't matter as long as I follow the guidance.

When your intuition becomes your primary source of guidance, you are always guided to the best result. This may not be the result you want, but it will be the one that will serve you in your future. When your mind is clear and quiet, it creates the space for expanded awareness and a clear channel to your guidance, which comes from your unconscious. I believe my intuition comes in when my unconscious becomes conscious—my blueprint reveals itself.

Much has been written about intuition and its source. I guess a person could just pick his or her favorite theory and continue living. It's easy to get distracted by various theories and the need to understand and know things. All you can do is to accept the invitation to move from surviving life, where you live by a set of rules and old patterns, and move to *living life* in accordance with your heart's desire. It doesn't mean avoiding all the painful experiences that will come. It only means you will continue to be given what you need to experience your soul's desire.

Developing Your Inner Witness

One tool that helps you listen to your guidance is monitoring your thinking. Continually check what your guidance has to say. Take note of where your mind spends the most time. Once you notice where your mind is—past, present, or future—you can begin to spend more time in the present. You know the past is behind you and cannot be changed. You also know you can only imagine or fantasize about the future.

When I ask a question about the future, I always get an answer like, "You will deal with whatever happens, so worrying about the future is a waste of time." I am not suggesting you don't plan your future from the perspective of bringing what you want into reality. I do suggest you don't obsess about the future.

Instead of worrying, obsessing, or fantasizing about the future, focus your energy on paying attention to your thinking. You will become a witness to your mental process, allowing you to take charge of your thinking and observe how your mind can jump to conclusions or react to a situation.

Your job is to bring your mind back to the present moment and watch what's going on within and outside you. This practice, of being your own witness, will bring you closer to developing the awareness necessary to notice when guidance shows up. You want your mind to be open enough to do what your guidance suggests.

You want to develop a new normal where you listen more and think less. When you are thinking, you are not listening. It's just like being in a conversation with someone. If you are thinking about what you are going to say next, you are not giving your full attention to the other person. Guidance is always available. You just have to learn to pay attention and then follow it. My history has taught me that my first impression is usually right. I suggest that you go back and review the times when you didn't follow your initial feeling or thought, and check out what you wish you had done.

Tapping into Your Guidance

Many people ask how to tap into their guidance. Guidance comes in many forms depending upon the individual. I will use intuition to illustrate how guidance comes into my awareness. I suggest that you begin to notice how your guidance shows up for you. Here are five ways to tap into your guidance.

1. *Recognize when you disregard intuition.*

This takes lots of practice because disregarding your intuition happens so fast. What I have noticed about myself might help you find out how your mind disregards your intuitive guidance.

Sometimes intuition comes as a nonverbal feeling. It's like getting a message I now have to act upon. I would ignore these messages because they were annoying. I shut off the link to my intuition and got into my head, where I thought too much. I made all kinds of excuses why I didn't have to follow my intuition to call a friend. I disregarded the guidance and came up with reasons not to call. I thought my phone call would interrupt him or he wouldn't be home, or any number of other reasons not to call. Fear of bothering people kept me from acting on my intuition.

I had been taught not to bother people. "Children should be seen and not heard," was my father's point of view. I grew up in a house where I had to avoid being punished physically. I learned to survive by squeezing into the behavioral box my parents demanded. Once I realized the origin of my fears, I was able to change my old belief that I was a bother. I no longer disregarded my intuitive impulse to contact someone.

It's time to sort out your childhood experiences. Start with limiting beliefs, and find their source. Discover your automatic thinking, and free yourself from habitual behaviors. You must create a new normal to fulfill your purpose—to follow your unconscious blueprint.

When your mind is in charge and does not like interruptions, you will label any inspiration as a distraction, automatically dismiss the guidance, and keep moving unconsciously through your day. Your mind is closed, with no room for new ideas to enter your awareness. Intuition is trying to get your attention, and you're not listening.

Imagine you're walking through the woods paying attention to the path in front of you. Your only goal is to get to where you are going. Your intuition is attempting to get you to slow down and experience the journey. Instead, you keep your head down with your attention fixed on the endpoint of your trip. It's like you're a horse running in a horserace with blinders preventing you from being distracted by life. In this case, you do not have to disregard intuition, because you're so closed that the light of intuition is kept out. While this might be an extreme example of being unconscious, it brings you to the first step in the transition to a new normal.

My first step in becoming conscious was to recognize I was wearing blinders. I had to take them off. I decided my life was more than getting to its endpoint with the least distraction. I decided to listen for intuitive guidance and pay attention so I could learn from my experiences. Once I was listening for intuitive guidance, I became aware of my surroundings and slowed down to enjoy the journey. Instead of fixating on a destination, I began to be more in the moment and lived the experience of each step

2. *Ask a question.*

Not knowing and asking a question is the key to opening your mind. A closed mind believes it knows everything, and there is no room for new information. Not knowing and asking is essential for making the space necessary to access your guidance. The act of asking a question causes you to stop thinking and listen. This creates the space for an answer. When the answer comes, leave it alone. Force yourself not to disregard it. Just sit with it and absorb the answer.

Rhetorical questions will not work because they are not real questions. They are statements in the form of a question. You think you know the answer, so new information will be blocked. The only question that works is one that comes from a place of honesty, without any underlying agenda. Become aware of the energy supporting the question. Make sure the words match the underlying energy. Communication is a form of energy, and the response you get is in response to the energy, as well as the words. If you believe you will always live alone and ask if there will ever be someone in your life, the answer will be no. The energy supporting the question will produce your *belief*—not what you want. Create your questions, believing you already have what you desire. It just hasn't materialized.

Ask your question from a place of not knowing and humility. Divinity, which is within your unconscious, will guide you. Some people experience ideas suddenly coming to mind. Others may experience just knowing without knowing how they know—they just know. Questions that promote your evolution and keep you on your journey are answered immediately—even before you can articulate the question. Questions are linear, and the response usually comes as a chunk of energy you must put into a linear form to add the words. I experience this kind of guidance as bolt of understanding that comes so fast I have to take a second to find the right words to describe what I received. The more you ask, the more you will reinforce the connections you have with the source of your guidance. Learn to always be connected to the source of your guidance. Constantly being aware of guidance will become a part of your new normal.

3.   *Practice asking for guidance in your everyday activities.*

Start with food selection. The next time you go to the supermarket, ask for guidance to select what it wants you to buy. Put yourself into the witness mode and see what happens. The more you use your guidance, the easier it will be for you to tap into it, and the easier it will be for your source of guidance to tap into you.

An example of being connected to your source of guidance is when you suddenly know it's time to leave the house for an appointment. After driving with all of the stoplights and slow drivers, you arrive at your destination to find the perfect parking spot. The really surprising part is when you walk into the meeting room, look at your watch, and see that you are exactly on time.

When you stop and look at this example, which has happened to me many times, you can see a pattern that I believe to be at the core of how life works—if you allow it!

Something motivated you to leave your house and get started toward your appointment. You know how to drive the car and negotiate the traffic. Synchronicity sets you up with all the necessary red or green lights, slow or fast drivers, and then provides you a perfect parking place. The interplay of intuition, or thoughts out of the blue, along with synchronicity is a beautiful thing.

4. *Meditate.*

When you meditate, you discover the benefit of being free from your mind's constant chatter. Meditation, along with guided imagery exercises and hypnosis, serve to suspend critical thinking. With critical thinking suspended, you are in the witness mode, which means your mind is in the audience and not at center stage.

There are many kinds of meditation. I suggest you find the kind of meditation that feels comfortable for you. I meditate while walking on a treadmill. I establish a comfortable walking speed, hold onto the side rails, and close my eyes. I start paying attention to my breathing. I imagine a pure white light coming into me on the in-breath. On the out-breath, I exhaust any negativity. Soon, both the in-breath and the out-breath are clear and white. The walking helps me control my weight and activates my brain to enhance mental efficiency. Take some time each day and meditate.

5. *Create space for guidance.*

I began my walking exercise one day, focusing on my heart and repeating a mantra, "I am walking with my soul." After ten minutes, I decided it wasn't working. I started repeating various phrases and noticed how I felt with each one. As the phrases became shorter and shorter, I just walked in silence. After five minutes of internal quiet, I became aware of my feet walking on the treadmill. Then I became aware of the pressure of my shirt on my shoulders, then the temperature of my back. My awareness was expanding. I was starting to get excited because something was definitely happening.

What happened next was very unexpected. I tried to ask a question about the future and got, "You'll know when the time comes." I tried to ask a question about my past and got, "The past is behind you." Then I couldn't even get the thought of a question to form in my mind before I became silent. I couldn't think. I went silent. I became awareness being aware of awareness.

While I think I understand the relationship between my intuition, mind, and synchronicity, that doesn't mean my life has automatically changed. If only it was that easy. Understanding by itself is not enough to change old behaviors. Behavior changes happen over time, as your new understanding takes over. In the meantime, you must practice bringing your mind into silence so you can spend more time listening. This step is critical to developing a new normal.

When you are functioning without thought, you are "in the zone." There is no thinking when you are in the zone. My granddaughter taught me a lot about being in the zone. After I watched a movie she made, I asked her why acting seemed to come so easy to her. She told me she memorizes her lines so well that when she is in a scene, she does not think; she moves through the scene in the persona of the character she is playing. I asked her how she came up with the idea to make, star in, edit, direct, and produce her movie. She said she was sitting around one day with nothing to do, and the idea just jumped into her head. The movie was so good; it amazed all who saw it. She was fifteen at the time. She was also sitting around with nothing occupying her mind, thus giving her guidance space to inspire. I don't recommend boredom as a way to tap into our guidance, but having nothing going on in our minds lowers the noise level so guidance can push through.

Anything you do begins with a clear intention. You must have enough discipline to clear your mind of anything restricting your ability to listen for intuitive messages or thoughts suddenly coming to mind. As you train yourself to seek out guidance, you will make your mind available to be guided.

The Big Question

"Why am I here?" is a common big question. As I have said, we are here for a reason. Instead of asking why you are here, ask for guidance to complete your journey and your life's purpose, which is to live the experience. Also, ask for the courage to take advantage of the opportunities synchronicity provides. Life is about living the mystery, showing up, and doing the best you can. You are on a journey that is taking you to every experience you need to fulfill your life's purpose. You don't have to worry about it. Knowing why life is what it is, or was what it was, is beyond your reach to understand, and it doesn't matter. How you label your journey doesn't change anything. The guidance you require will always be given. Synchronicity will always be creating opportunities, regardless of what you do, or don't do, to participate in the experience.

Guidance and Synchronicity

Guidance provides you a direction. Then you can align your resources accordingly. Now you are on your way, with a clear direction to fulfill your purpose. All you need now is a set of coincidences that create the opportunities for you to experience. Enter synchronicity. You cannot influence synchronicity. You cannot create it or stop it from happening. While you can refuse to follow your guidance, you cannot prevent synchronicity from creating opportunities for you.

When a client suggested I write about my experiences as a mental health therapist working in a jail, the seed was planted for my first book, *Coming Together, Healing Body, Mind and Spirit*. My first job as a clinical social worker was with the Arlington County Department of Human Services (DHS). I was assigned to the detention facility (jail), where I met the most interesting people. Many of the inmates were there because of underlying mental health problems. The ten years I worked in the jail provided me the opportunity to be of service to a very wounded population, and I learned a great deal about the effects of trauma.

The inspiration for my second book came as the result of my sitting at a card table at Staples, showcasing my first book. A lady stopped on her way out of the store and bought a book. Six months later, I received a call from her. She had just read the book and wanted to meet with me.

She came to my office and said, "You are supposed to write another book."

"Why?" I asked. She had no idea. With the message delivered, the meeting came to an end.

Meeting with this lady was an example of how opportunities show up. This is how the universe works. An opportunity will show up, and we can choose to accept the challenge. Pursuing her suggestion resulted in my second book, *Intuition: Pathway to Destiny.*

Fast forward. I am a guest at a conference on coaching in San Diego. As I waited for the conference room doors to open, a man I had met the day before approached me, announcing, "We are supposed to write a book together."

Here we go again. The universe is calling. An opportunity presented itself, and I said yes.

This book was written because I agreed to show up and experience what was going to unfold. The circumstance of our meeting and having similar beliefs and interests was a remarkable coincidence. We met over lunch a few times and worked out the details of coauthoring a book. I was to write the front half and he the second half. I simply showed up and did my best. The ideas and inspirations came to me, and I was the scribe. Thanks to Gregory Reese Smith for stepping up and offering me the opportunity to work with him. Otherwise, nothing would have happened, and I would have missed out on the experience of writing this book.

Gregory and I wrote our contributions to what we thought would be our book and then decided to take what we had written and continue to develop our ideas. I set aside what I had written for months, not knowing where it was going. I needed guidance. The awaited guidance came during a casual conversation with a good friend about the book. I was ruminating about how I was stuck. I knew the book wasn't finished, but I didn't know where to go with it. I was talking about how I live life as a spiritual being having a life experience, and suddenly I knew the direction of the book. I decided to help others who are ready to create a new normal. Synchronicity brought Gregory into my life to get me started on this book.

Another synchronicity story is about how a British sound engineer came out of nowhere to solve a Department of Defense problem with military funeral honors. The story began in my kitchen, where I had just finished breakfast. My wife, Meg Falk, was commenting on an article in the *Washington Post* about how there were not enough buglers in the military needed to sound "Taps" at military funerals. Meg thought "we" could do better.

Meg was the director of the Office of Family Policy that included having policy responsibility for military funeral honors. There was a problem due to a shortage of buglers to sound "Taps." Here is her story in her own words:

> One of my casualty policy responsibilities as director of family policy for the secretary of defense was military funeral honors. In the late 1990s, as many as twelve thousand World

War II veterans were dying each day, and the military force was downsizing. As a result, when family members wanted funeral honors for their veteran, the military services often were unable to provide them due to lack of personnel. The Veterans Service Organizations (VSOs) were very displeased with the Department of Defense for not providing this service. So we decided that instead of going head-to-head with the VSOs, we would invite them to collaborate with us on a solution. After many meetings and focus groups on the issue, we agreed that the most important elements of funeral honors were the folding and presentation of the flag and the sounding of "Taps." We likewise agreed that at least one member of the military funeral group should be from the branch of service in which the veteran served. In addition, we received authority for the reserves to help with this effort. All requests would be honored and handled by the services through a toll-free number, when requested by the family through their funeral director. Seemingly, the problem was solved.

My gut was telling me that the problem was not solved. The dignified delivery of funeral honors was marred by the fact that real buglers were not available for most veterans' funerals because "Taps" was played by a boom box. The tapes used were often scratched and lacked quality sound. My intuition told me there had to be a better way.

I thought that with modern technology, we could come up with some sort of digital bugle that would sound "Taps" even though the person holding it did not know how to play a bugle. This would significantly elevate the dignity of the funeral honors ceremony. When I floated this idea up the chain, I was told it was a crazy idea, probably not possible, that it wasn't worth the effort, and that veterans' families would feel deceived. My instinct told me otherwise, so I went under the radar to pursue this "crazy" concept.

Working with our contractor, Tony Minor, I asked him to get in touch with major sound companies to see if they were interested in developing something like this. None of them were. I asked Tony to keep on trying. Coincidentally, he was meeting with a friend of his in New York and told him what I wanted to be developed.

His friend, Simon Britt, from the UK, turned out to be a sound engineer who said, "Let me take a look at it."

Fast forward. Simon developed a prototype bugle that played "Taps" digitally, and some months later we demonstrated it at the Pentagon. Several of my superiors were still a bit dubious about the veterans' families and VSOs accepting it. Nonetheless, they asked Simon to go back and make a few improvements. I deliberately kept all of these plans quiet as my gut was telling me that once the word of the bugle got out, everyone would want one immediately. I was right.

We held a big meeting with all the VSOs, and part of that meeting included the premiering of the ceremonial bugle. We first brought in the premier bugler from Arlington National Cemetery, who played "Taps" on a real bugle. Then we brought out the ceremonial bugle, and it, too, sounded "Taps" perfectly. The crowd went wild. As I expected, they all wanted one right away.

The innovation of the ceremonial bugle was featured on local news and national media.

When people in England found out about it, they contacted Simon and asked him, "What are you going to do for the homeland?"

As a result, all countries in the Commonwealth now have ceremonial bugles that sound "Last Post," which is their "Taps."

The most rewarding thing about all of this is that now thousands of veterans' funeral honors ceremonies all over the world are more dignified and give greater respect to those who served their nations.

Following one's instinct, in spite of doubts all around, can result in large rewards for many. In this case, it is our veterans who are so deserving of dignity and respect at their funerals.

**

Was it just coincidence Meg happened to be in the right job at the right time to take the initiative to resolve this problem? Was it coincidence Simon had lunch with Tony Minor? I believe this was synchronicity at work.

Summary

Evolution is all about change. In this case, it's about fulfilling your purpose by creating a new normal. You can create a new normal to evolve from living on automatic to living consciously. You can become aware of the guidance available to direct you to the experiences you need to evolve and fulfill your soul's desire.

Life has a purpose. You are not here by accident. You are a contributor to, and collaborator in, a larger scheme that's beyond your understanding. You are here to evolve from developing your survival skills to developing your ability to communicate with the source of your guidance.

Think of yourself as an explorer who has been given a map with all the information needed to embark on a journey of a lifetime. All you need to get started is the courage to follow your guidance. Once you commit to the journey, synchronicity will provide the opportunities.

While you are creating your new normal, you will discover you are becoming much more than what you thought you were. You are not an identity. You are evolving beyond the need to hang your hat on any identity. If you really need an identity, try on being a soul having a life experience.

CHAPTER 2

Preparation

Show up and do your best. You are prepared for the challenge.

On September 11, 2001, I was working in my office on the eleventh floor of the Arlington County Detention Facility when a friend stuck his head into my office and told me a plane had just flown into the World Trade Center. I assumed it was a small plane and continued working. A few minutes later, I decided to see what was going on and went into the cafeteria, where there was a TV. The first thing I noticed was smoke coming from one of the towers. Then I saw an airliner fly into the adjacent tower. It took a second to take in what I saw. I thought, *We're under attack.* I was frozen in front of the TV. I stood spellbound for several minutes before going back to my office, where I saw the red message light flashing on my phone.

I picked up the receiver and punched in the code to retrieve my messages. What I heard is still echoing in my memory. "Jim, no matter what you see or what you hear, I'm all right."

Flight 77 had just flown into the Pentagon, where Meg was holding a meeting. I felt like I had been shot at and missed.

During Meg's years at the Pentagon, she would join the other smokers at ground zero in the center of the building. She would tell the story of how one day she saw a plane flying over going from or to National Airport, she thought that if a plane ever hit the building, the first thing she would do was contact me and let me know she was all right. She learned this from her friend Sharon Bryson, who, at the time, headed the Family Assistance Office at the National Transportation Safety Board (NTSB). In the course of one of their dinners together, Sharon told Meg that all airlines require their employees, whether they are ticket takers or baggage handlers, to call home immediately if there ever is a plane crash. This was to prevent airline family members from clogging up the phone lines. The memory of this conversation came back to Meg on 9/11. As it turned out for Meg and her staff, letting their loved ones know they were all right before they left the building prevented a lot of grief and worry. I can attest to that!

What unfolded for the rest of that day and the days to come is an example of how the universe prepares us for extraordinary situations. The conversations we have had with friends and colleagues, the experiences we carry with us without even being aware of what we know, come into play.

I was the proverbial fly on the wall as Meg, the director of the Office of Family Policy for the secretary of defense, showed up on 9/11 and went into action. She knew she had to create a family assistance center for the family members who lost loved ones in the Pentagon and on flight 77. While Meg was going into action, I was still shaken by nearly losing my wife. I started calling her family and friends to let them know she was alive I finished the third call before the phone would only produce a busy signal. While I couldn't call out, I could apparently receive calls because Meg called me and asked me to get in touch with the county manager because she needed his help to find the space required to set up a center. *Coincidentally*, the only person I know in the manager's office answered the phone. She knew I was credible when I told her I was calling on behalf of the Defense Department and needed the county's help to establish a place where family members could receive the support they need. She did not hesitate to take Meg's contact information and do what was necessary to meet Meg's needs. Luckily, the person who contacted Meg knew the manager of the Sheraton Hotel in Crystal City, who made his hotel available on a handshake.

Meg tells the story of how, after calling me, she and some of her staff evacuated the building and set up shop in an air force office, where she started locating key Pentagon staff. In all of the chaos following the attack, Meg was able to reach the people who were critical to setting up a family assistance center. I thought it was amazing that those she had to talk to actually answered the phone. When does that ever happen?

Meg got permission to set up the family assistance center and was told to have it functioning by the next day. Imagine being told to find a location and create a complex operation and have it functioning within literally hours. Here is where being prepared comes into play. Not that anyone could purposely prepare for such an event as 9/11. Preparations had been happening over a lifetime and were orchestrated by forces beyond our imagination.

Meg learned about how to take over a hotel from Sharon Bryson, who told her about keeping media from intruding on the families, holding two briefings a day, and allowing families to go to the site where their loved one perished. All of these shared practices came to mind during decision making on 9/11. As an example, Meg intuitively knew to avoid establishing the center on a military installation because security would be too tight, and many of the affected families would not be able to access the center if they lacked proper ID.

The morning after the attack, Meg and I were talking about what to call the center. We bounced around several names while she was drying her hair, and suddenly she said, "Call the hotel and have them connect you with the people setting up the center. Tell whoever answers that the center will be referred to as the Pentagon Family Assistance Center (PFAC)."

I called the hotel and was connected to someone I knew from Meg's office. What a coincidence! I passed along Meg's message naming the center and asked how close they were to being operational. He said the telephone company was setting up the phone, and they should be done before seven o'clock that morning.

I made Meg's breakfast (a fried egg on toast, which is the only thing I know how to cook), and she was off to the Pentagon briefing. She stopped at the door, turned around, and said, "I don't know what I'm doing."

I said, "You'll know when you need to know." And she was out the door.

As I think about it now, I realize that while I was intending to send her off with a word of encouragement, I was also telling her what was about to happen. She was already prepared for this day.

In Meg's account of 9/11, she wrote,

> To this day, I look back and am astonished that the decisions we made on 9/11 would turn out to be exactly what was needed. On that awful day, I was also inspired to call the Norfolk Family Service Center for assistance as they, unfortunately, had gone through the experience of setting up a family assistance center the prior year in the aftermath of the USS *Cole* bombing. Fortunately, the director of the center was my good friend and colleague Cathy Stokoe. She and six staff drove up that night to assist. They

were critical in our ability to set up the center overnight.

The next morning at seven o'clock, there were forty volunteers from the Pentagon setting up and staffing the center. I announced the opening of the Pentagon Family Assistance Center (PFAC) at the Pentagon briefing on September 12, and the families of the missing started to come. With the wide range of organizational support right there at the PFAC, the grieving families did not have to go around to all these organizations for assistance. The support services were all in one place for them, making the agony of their loss much less burdensome.

As I look back from my current perspective, I wonder how Meg did it. How could one person accomplish what she did in the hours following the attack? Meg was not only the right person for the job; she was the only person for the job. I know I'm just a little prejudiced, but look at the facts.

Meg began her career with the military working as a program manager for the navy's family service centers (FSCs), where she became a subject matter expert. She was asked to move from the navy to the Office of the Secretary of Defense (OSD), where she became the director of the Office of Family Policy and had policy responsibilities for military family support, casualty assistance, and mortuary affairs. She was in the right place at the right time.

She met her counterparts who had mass casualty responsibilities for the NTSB and FBI, where she learned about how they did their jobs.

She had thought about what she would do if a plane crashed into the building years before it happened.

She developed friendships with people who just happened to be in positions to assist her, like Cathy Stokoe, who, along with her team from Norfolk, drove through the night to have the PFAC operational when the first family members began to arrive.

Summing up Meg's account of 9/11, she writes,

> As word of the PFAC spread, even more family members started to show up. Also, the casualty assistance officers assigned to the military and civilian families and the families of those on flight 77 arrived to help. We briefed the families twice a day. Sometimes there would be hundreds of people in the ballroom during the briefings. It was the one place families could go where they knew they would receive accurate information, as there were many false rumors during those dark days. Other organizations (e.g., Therapy Dogs, Red Cross) also started arriving to assist, and we had virtually every possible type of support available for the families on site. As my husband often reminds me, "You had a great idea, and it is a good thing so many showed up to save your butt." Very true.
>
> The PFAC was a supportive, safe haven for those experiencing the worst loss of their lives. As one young son said to the child care staff, "I like being here. You understand what I am going through."
>
> We operated the PFAC 24–7 for a month. My experience at the center was the most intense time of my life.

As I look back, I see that so many experiences, colleagues, and friends prepared me for that tragic day in American history. The lessons I culled from previous DoD mass casualty incidents helped form in my mind what we needed to do immediately. The best practices and lessons learned from my colleagues at the NTSB, the FBI, and the Military Service Family Centers profoundly influenced the decisions made and actions taken in establishing and running the PFAC. My direct interaction with the families from the 1996 CT-43 plane crash in Croatia that killed the Commerce Secretary Ron Brown and thirty-four others taught me to always keep the families first—the guiding principle of the PFAC. The CT-43 families also taught me that each person handles grief and loss in his or her own way. No two people grieve the same.

It was during the meetings with the CT-43 families that I met my good friend Kathryn Turman, director of victim assistance for the FBI. Through the years, Kathryn has shared with me many lessons learned on how best to assist victims of violence and terrorism. I watched how she interacted with the families of the victims from Black Hawk Down in Somalia, Pan Am 103, and Khobar Towers, to name a few. She is always the compassionate professional, keeping the families first, and she is exquisitely sensitive to the many needs of victims' families. All of these influences and experiences came to bear on that fateful day and for the duration of the PFAC.

I am grateful to all those who have gifted me along the way with their wisdom and willingness to pass on their lessons learned. What they shared with me played an essential role in my ability to be in the zone and listen to my intuition following the 9/11 Pentagon attack.

Meg's account of her taking charge and developing a plan to address the tragedy on 9/11 is an example of how well she was prepared to go into action. Previous experiences, along with information she gained from her good friends at the FBI and the NTSB, all came into play.

We can see the sequence of events as a series of coincidences, or synchronicity at work, or look at it all from a different perspective—a perspective that there are no coincidences because everything unfolded as planned. Meg said it best when she recalled being in the zone. Anyone who has experienced being in the zone knows that thinking gets in the way. One is operating beyond thought, where answers flow from a place of knowing.

CHAPTER 3

Prepare Yourself

Start preparing yourself to be your best by getting out of your way. Fear is usually what gets in the way. You fear mistakes, what others may think, or the unknown. What helped me was to not overthink a situation.

I discovered I did not have to believe I was alone. I could relax and allow myself to be guided. This was the tipping point between a life lived within the limits of my mind and a life lived in partnership with the divine. I no longer expected to know things I was never designed to know. I felt a weight lift from me as I told my mind and ego they were no longer expected to know things such as what I should do in every situation, or being in control all the time. I learned I couldn't really keep myself, or anyone else, safe or know what the best thing was to do. Who do you want to trust with your life? Do you want to trust your limited mind, or do you want to create your new normal with the help of the divine? I discovered I was far better off trusting the divine and following my intuition.

Resolving Past Events and Limiting Beliefs

Most of us start off a little insecure, so we look for something outside of ourselves to make us feel better. I remember that owning my own car was a big deal for me. My first car was a 1949 Chevy. It wasn't "cool" enough, so I bought a 1958 Corvette. I would pick up my girlfriend at her high school and feel like I was somebody. All the while, of course, I really knew I wasn't anybody, because I was taught that as a kid. My older sister constantly reminded me I was stupid. She resented me because I had destroyed her life as an only child. She liked all the attention, and then I came along.

The point of my story is to illustrate how the past can be traumatic and create a limiting belief. The simplest event can create a limiting belief that remains with you until it's discovered and replaced by the truth. My belief that I was stupid was dismantled when I completed graduate school. I updated my limiting belief to match reality. The dismantling happened when I replaced my limiting belief with the fact that I was smart enough to complete graduate school. The old, limiting belief could not continue in the light of the facts.

You're born with a fear-based operating system designed to keep you alive and to seek comfort while avoiding discomfort. Your mind operates from a rational point of view. Your instincts and intuition have no fear and are not constrained by your experiences. Everyone is influenced by events in their past that created limiting beliefs that keep them from exercising free will and free choice.

If you are going to be able to show up and do your best, you have to be able to exercise free will and free choice. Obstructions to exercising free will and free choice are found among your limiting beliefs. Here is where your search for psychological freedom begins. You learned limiting beliefs in childhood, and they are inaccurate. You are born knowing that you are unable to protect yourself and need to rely on others for survival. If you learn you are safe in the world, you develop differently from someone who learns life is unsafe. Your goal is to teach yourself what you experienced as a child is in the past. While you cannot change the past, you can create a new understanding about what happened.

Your challenge is to accept the fact that you never got all you needed and to realize you cannot resolve the past by looking outside of yourself. Accept the reality of the past and shift from seeking what you need from others to finding everything you need within yourself. When you make this shift, you will create a new normal.

The way you identify a past event that needs your attention, or change a limiting belief, is to notice how you respond to a situation. If you overreact to something on television or to a situation that causes you to react very emotionally, you have work to do. The opposite of overreacting is to underreact. If you find yourself not reacting when all those around you are, you have work to do. Welcome these situations as an opportunity to resolve past trauma.

Memories that rent space in your head are another indicator of events that need resolution. Develop the ability to be aware of your emotions by listening to what's going on moment by moment. Notice when a reaction is out of balance with the situation. Observe the reaction that is out of balance, and ask yourself, "Why?" Follow the reaction back in time to discover what happened. This is how you unearth your demons, slay your dragons, stand free of your past, and are unafraid of the future. When you are no longer constrained by your past, you are on your way to creating your new normal.

If you want to be unafraid, you must replace your old way of staying safe with a more powerful one. Your old way was based on the myth that you were in control, and you were smart and strong enough to keep yourself safe. When you discover you are not equipped to do what you expect, you can surrender your old beliefs and allow a more powerful source to keep you safe. This transition begins by learning to trust that if you follow your guidance, you will be safe and have everything you need. In fact, you will discover you have no needs at all. You will learn you have nothing to prove.

As you become more secure within yourself, you can be in a very loving relationship without contorting yourself, because the relationship will not be based on need. Needs are temporary, as are those kinds of relationships. Love-based relationships need nothing beyond the authenticity of the other, because no unconscious needs are searching for satisfaction.

The process of getting out of your way includes doing the work that shows up. There will be unfinished business that must be worked through and brought to a resolution so nothing stands in the way of reaching your potential.

Managing Your Thinking and Focusing Your Awareness

Learning how to manage your thinking and focusing your awareness is part of getting out of your way.

Why must you manage your thinking? When your chatterbox mind is engaged, you have virtually no awareness, which limits your possibilities. Thinking takes up all of the space needed to sense your intuition. You will discover the less *chatterbox* thinking the better. Becoming aware requires you to stop thinking too much and listen. Awareness only exists at the moment, so if you are in your head thinking away, you cannot be aware of anything else. You will only be able to hear your own thoughts.

Just as you manage your chatterbox mind, you want to focus your awareness. Your goal is to be aware of where your awareness is and where you want it to be. Part of awareness is to have the ability to observe yourself. You have to see yourself before you can change yourself. You also must take responsibility for your thinking. Without the discipline to stop your unconscious ways, you will continue living like you were in the movie *Groundhog Day,* which is a movie about a news reporter who has to live the same day over and over.

Another part of awareness is to develop your ability to constantly listen for guidance. Being aware allows you to notice what your awareness is noticing. Awareness begins when you are quiet and listening.

Awareness can be focused like a beam of light on a single activity, like when you are driving past a large truck at night in heavy rain. You are not thinking about anything except what is going on right in front of you. Continuing with the driving example, when the road is clear and the weather nice and sunny, you can become aware of your surroundings and enjoy the ride. Your awareness can expand to the full extent of your senses when you are not driving and can sit back and relax. One day as I sat next to the pond in my backyard, I could hear birds, the pond's waterfall, the sound of the mail truck, an airliner passing overhead, and a dog barking in the distance. You are able to take in and be aware of all of your senses when you are still.

Awareness Practices

Here are some practices you can do to focus your awareness. Start by noticing your thoughts and how your emotions follow along. Emotion always follows a thought, so you can learn the cause of an emotion by searching for its underlying thought.

You have a choice of whether to keep thinking thoughts that cause you to be uncomfortable or decide to think more constructive thoughts that will bring you back to the intuitive level of functioning. Awareness will help manage your thinking so you can enjoy the benefits: tranquility and being in a relaxed state of mind. This all takes discipline to keep your mind on task.

Your mind is not used to being on task. It's used to wandering all over the place with no particular mission. You are taking charge and stopping the inner chatter when you put your mind to work. You are taking charge and giving your mind an expanded mission with awareness as a tool. You know being in the moment is important, though it's hard to stay in the moment. You will get bored and want to get going into the future with your fantasies or into the past with your assumptions about what happened. Recognize this process and prevent it by stopping your automatic thinking. Force yourself to provide a new job for your mind—the job of becoming more aware.

Trusting Intuition

I learned that the faster I run through all my solutions and decide there are solutions I haven't thought of, the less time I spend mulling over the problem. I go directly to *not knowing* and asking. You are left with following your gut in situations where there just isn't enough time to think through a problem.

I was confronted with a home maintenance problem. I found water on the basement floor. Water was coming out from under the furnace. I thought it must have been coming from the humidifier, so I shut off the water. I still had the problem. Then I took the front panels off of the furnace and looked inside. I found a puddle of water under the fan motor and figured the drain line must have been plugged. I decided to call the company that put in the furnace. I knew what was wrong, and I also knew I wasn't going to be able to do the repairs. I gave up.

After giving up, I was inspired to look at the installation manual. Reading the directions is always a good idea. It was like a foreign language, so I found myself just staring at all of the hoses, pipes, and mechanisms.

I said to myself, "What do I do now?"

Then I saw a rusty spot on the bottom of the unit. Then I saw a drop of water drip from one of the hoses. Eureka—I found a broken hose clamp was allowing water to leak from the drain system. I replaced the clamp. When I stopped thinking and got out of my way, I saw what I needed to see.

As you free yourself from past conditioning, you will become confident your future will be taken care of, and you will fulfill your purpose. You will rely on your intuition and be comfortable in the moment. If you develop a partnership with your intuition, you will navigate through the opportunities provided by synchronicity that will get your attention in some way. That's why it is important to notice what you notice.

It's critical to learn to pay attention to what you notice, because you notice things for a reason. Practice acting on what you notice. I acted on a public service announcement asking for volunteers at my local hospice. I noticed the ad for some reason. Acting on what I noticed changed my life. My retirement from the navy was only two years away, and I was looking for my next career. I didn't know what I wanted to do next. I joked that I didn't know who I wanted to be when I grew up. I liked the hospice experience so much that I became a clinical social worker. This is how my soul's blueprint works. My becoming a social worker was imprinted within my soul. That's why I noticed the public service announcement. I simply got out of my own way and allowed the rest to unfold.

Being aware of awareness is like noticing what you notice. Once you notice something, like a public service announcement, you have the opportunity to make a decision that might change your life. You cannot know at the time whether you are doing the right thing or what impact your decision will have. The sooner you learn there are things you will never know, the easier it will be to trust intuition will never steer you off course.

Learn how to surrender your need to know. Most of the time knowing is not required, because the answer will be available to you when you stop thinking and ask. Start out by trying to use your logic and rational thinking to come up with an answer. Think about what to do until you give up and ask. The problem is you are only able to find solutions from what you know. These solutions are limited by your personal knowledge and experience.

Summarizing Ideas

Totally enjoy the minute-by-minute experience of life. This is how to fulfill your purpose.

Treat life like a journey. Journeys provide discoveries that are necessary for evolution. You are invited to journey beyond the known—beyond the horizon of knowledge. Your journey has no destination. You will never get to where you are going, because there is no end to life, when you consider life as your soul's journey. Maybe that's the point. It's an unfolding process that never ends.

Life experiences give you every opportunity to successfully fulfill your purpose. If you don't do anything, nothing happens. You live, survive, and then you die. So what? A life should not be wasted. It's so precious. So what are you supposed to do? Recognize what your mind is capable of doing. It's designed to solve problems and accomplish tasks. It's designed to ponder complicated problems and do the math. It's not designed to know the future. It is designed to receive information from outside of itself. That's how Albert Einstein came up with his E=MC² formula. He said the formula came to him and was not a product of his thinking. This is where you are headed, consciously creating the space for inspiration to enter your mind—to have thoughts out of the blue.

You can decide to participate in the evolution from a traditional normal to consciously following your internal blueprint. Your self-concept will expand. You will be in an all-inclusive group where you are united as part of the whole. You will be invited to follow the path that arrives in front of you. The only thing standing in your way is you.

Like most people, you're projecting your past into the future. Your goal is to stop limiting yourself by your past but to seek and create the unimaginable. When you create, you're creating in accordance with your divine path. Your journey is given to you as a way to have a purpose and a path to follow. The solution to all of your questions is to be still and listen. Be still and allow creation to become present. Then go into action.

The goal is the unification of your plan with your divine path—your blueprint. How do you do that? Start where you are with the intention to remove any restrictions between you and your potential. Restrictions are found in your body, mind, and spirit. You need a good spring housecleaning. Open all the windows, pull back the furniture, and get under the rugs. The purpose of the cleaning is to find and resolve restrictions found in all aspects of life—body, mind, and spirit.

CHAPTER 4

Healing Your Body

Our bodies store emotional and physical trauma that we have not processed. If something happens that is so deeply traumatic that we are unable to digest it, the trauma gets stored in our bodies. Resolving unprocessed trauma eliminates symptoms caused by an event that has been stored within the fabric of our physiology.

Jane's Surgery

Jane had been through several operations for the removal of cancerous tumors in her right leg, left arm, and stomach. She was in pain after the surgery, feeling that her body had gone through a shock. She thought she needed help to heal.

I explained how we could learn what was needed to help her heal. I described how I would set up a way for her to communicate with her various incisions through guided imagery, the use of her imagination. Her goal was to communicate directly with her body to learn what was needed to help her heal.

I told her, "Thinking isn't required. What you are going to do is not within your mind's capabilities. Your mind is designed to think things through and accomplish complicated tasks."

The guided imagery began as I invited her to become relaxed and allow my words to guide her through the experience. She had done this kind of work before and was able to allow her mind to relax and watch. She leaned back on the couch, closed her eyes, and took a deep breath.

The following is an account of the guided imagery I used to resolve the presenting problem:

> Me: Picture or imagine walking along a boardwalk at the beach. It's a beautiful day. The sky is the perfect color blue. There are puffy white clouds perfectly contrasted against the bright blue sky. The breeze is blowing softly through your hair, and you can smell the aromas from the food stands along the boardwalk. Up ahead, you notice there is a stairway leading from the boardwalk down to the beach. There are ten steps in all. In a moment, you are going to descend the stairs, as I count from one to ten. With each number I say, you will become more and more relaxed until, at the count of ten, you will be at the perfect level of relaxation to do the healing you want to do.
>
> Now begin to descend the stairs as I count them off. One ... two ... three, becoming more and more relaxed, four ... five, halfway to being at the perfect level of relaxation, six ... seven, more and more relaxed, eight ... nine, almost there, and ten, at the perfect level of relaxation.
>
> As you step away from the stairs, you notice how the sand feels under your feet. It's the perfect

temperature. You walk along the beach, noticing we are really all alone; there is no one to bother us, and we have all the time we need.

You see a beach chair up ahead and decide to sit down and relax even more. Make yourself comfortable; enjoy this perfect level of relaxation. Your body enjoys being so relaxed. Your blood is flowing easily through all parts of your body. Your nervous system is relaxed and functioning perfectly. Every part of your body is getting just what it needs and wants. To heal even faster, you are going to invite the parts of your body that have been operated on recently to express just how they feel and what they want to heal even faster.

Beginning with the incision on your right leg, take your imagination to that place and ask how it's feeling.

Jane: It feels scared. It doesn't know if it's safe or if more pain is coming at any moment.

Me: Be with this part for a moment and tell it the truth. When it knows that no more operations are scheduled or expected, then ask it what it needs to heal quickly and easily.

Jane: It knows the truth now.

Me: Ask what it needs to heal quickly and easily.

Jane: It doesn't know what it needs.

Me: Okay. Ask if your unconscious knows what is needed to help this part heal. Then send the energy to the wounded area in the form of colored light.

Jane: I'm sending it green light from my heart.

Me: Good. Let the most perfect green light fill and surround the wound on your leg. Ask all parts of your body to support this healing in the most perfect way. When the area on your leg is full of green light, and it seems like you are finished with your leg, ask your leg how it's doing.

Jane: It's more relaxed—more comfortable.

Me: Now, move your awareness to your right arm and ask what it's experiencing.

Jane: My arm told me to do less, but I don't know what that means.

Me: So let's find out. Imagine sitting in the center of a very large movie theater. There are large screens all around you, and you are going to be shown just what your arm is trying to tell you. Communication at this level of mind is always symbolic. In the metaphors, you may see several pictures. Notice what stands out. In a moment, I'm going to count from one to three. At the count of three, your unconscious will give you all the pictures you need to understand what the wound on your arm is telling you. One … two … three.

Jane (after several minutes): I saw many pictures, but the one that stood out the most was of a man climbing up a hill and a small child running down the hill as he was playing with a hoop and a stick.

Me: Ask what it means.

Jane: Life is a matter of choices. I can either work hard at being good, or play as a child. It really doesn't matter. I saw myself in ancient combat. I was holding a child in one hand and flowers in the other. It's all a matter of choice.

Me: And what do you choose?

Jane: I guess I can lighten up and slow down.

Me: Excellent. Now, just as before, ask the arm what it needs to heal quickly and easily. Find whatever it needs within you, and send it to the wounded area in the form of colored light. I'll wait until you're finished. When you're done, and take all the time you need, move to your stomach and ask what it's experiencing.

Jane (five minutes later): My stomach thinks the surgery wasn't necessary and is angry with me.

Me: Did you have some moles removed?

Jane: Yes, my doctor thought they might cause problems in the future.

Me: Send the memory of your doctor telling you why surgery was necessary to your stomach incisions. I doubt if your stomach was listening at the time of your consultation with the doctor. Once your stomach knows why the surgery was necessary, bring the perfect light and healing energy from within your body to your stomach until you sense all is in balance.

Jane (two minutes later): I'm done.

Me: Then bring yourself back to full alertness, and let's talk about what just happened.

We talked about her experience. I explained that the body knows no time, and her body didn't have the big picture.

"You may have two arms and two legs, but I'm not sure they talk to one another," I said to her. "You know the old story about the right hand not knowing what the left hand is doing? It could be true. The right hand may not know what the left hand is doing. It's up to you to keep your body in balance by communicating with all of its parts. This is done through proper energy flow within your body. We don't want any of your parts to be orphaned."

The techniques used in this example included communicating with parts of Jane's body and moving energy in the form of light. The body, mind, and spirit don't respond to complex thoughts or ideas. They do respond to objects and images—which is why you dream in objects and images. The objects in dreams are metaphors, poetic representations. It's a mistake to think dreaming about your neighbor represents something about the neighbor as a person. What is really happening is your unconscious just picked the neighbor as a symbol of thoughts or feelings the neighbor may have triggered in you.

I remember dreaming about being unable to find my next classroom in high school. When I woke, I knew I wasn't really dreaming about being unable to find my next class in school, because I hadn't been in school or a classroom for fifteen years or more. The dream must have meant something else, such as expressing my fear of not being where I should be or getting lost.

I used guided imagery with Jane to put her mind into a dream state. Once in the dream state, her conscious mind was comfortable just observing, while her unconscious took over. Jane's conscious mind had to understand what the pictures meant. Once she received and understood the message, she was able to make some changes. In this story, it was all right for Jane to accomplish less and still be a good person. The message came by way of the wound on her arm.

In the weeks and months that followed, Jane found she was working at a more comfortable pace. She even hired someone to help out in her office. Her wounds healed nicely, with little discomfort.

Disharmony affects how your body functions. Even the finest violin needs tuning. Notice the harmony and rhythm of your body. If you don't, it will do what it needs to do to get your attention.

Body Memories

I've selected some stories of how the body not only stores your history but also acts as a repository of past physical and emotional trauma.

Frank experienced significant abuse from his father. One day he came to therapy and showed me a scar on his leg that had begun to bleed. He didn't know why it started to bleed; it just did. We decided to see if he could remember what caused the scar. With a little help, he remembered his father burning his leg with a cigarette—because Frank had brought him the wrong tool. He did not know what a ten-inch crescent wrench was and brought his father something else. For this transgression, his father burned him on his leg. Once the memory of being burned was brought out into the open, the scar stopped bleeding, and Frank could recall the event as just another time his father hurt him.

Patterns in one's life can be indicators of unfinished business from a previous life. The following story is an example of how healing can take place in any setting. This healing all happened in thirty minutes.

I was offering demonstrations on energy healing in a booth set up at the Maryland Psychic Fair. I had never demonstrated my techniques in public. I tried not to show how I felt, which was nervous. I used a massage table and a pendulum to scan the body's energy system. Many people just wanted to talk about energy healing until a middle-aged man approached, accompanied by his wife and daughter. Their black t-shirts, long hair, and heavy boots made me think they were members of a motorcycle club. I must admit, their appearance added to my anxiety. He told me he had a history of chronic back pain.

I invited him to lie down on his stomach and began to scan his back where he said he was in pain. I asked him to put his imagination into the area of his back that was giving him trouble. Rhythmic music was playing at a Native American booth adjacent to mine. The drumming and flute melodies surrounded us as he became silent and imagined going into the small of his back.

Before long, he described watching a cannonball rip through a man, killing him instantly. The scene was from our Revolutionary War, a battle going on, and a cannonball went right through the same area of the man's back that was giving him all the trouble. He said he thought his pain was caused by a recent fall from the roof of a house. He was a roofer and had fallen several times, injuring his back in the same place. It was as though he was being sent hints directing him to investigate the source of some unfinished business.

Sometimes when people suffer a violent death, some of their spirit energy gets split off and is left behind. A way to find out whether some spirit was left behind is to ask the question. Since the conscious mind isn't equipped to know, I have to ask the unconscious mind. I asked him to look around the battle area and see if any of the man's spirit had been split off or fragmented when the cannonball went through him.

I told him to ask his unconscious if any of his spirit was split off during this death. He asked the question, and a thought came to him that he needed to have a fragmented piece of his spirit back. The easiest way to bring back a piece spirit that has been split off is to ask it if it is willing to go to where it belongs. He asked if it was okay for him to gather up what belonged to him and return to this day and time. He imagined gathering up the spirit that had been split off and returned to normal awareness.

Were the accidents to his back coincidental? Was his unconscious causing him to fall off of roofs as a message to pay more attention to his back? When I asked my unconscious the question, the answer was immediate and clear. There is no such thing as a coincidence.

This story shows how fragmented spirit energy can be brought from the past and integrated into the body. The connection between body and mind was played out in an effort to resolve a past trauma.

I can only wonder how many people carry wounds still stored in their body, waiting for the right time to surface. Was it a coincidence that he found me at the Maryland Psychic Fair? Not likely. Such is the magic of life.

About Ann—Healing Body, Mind, and Spirit

Ann was born in England before World War II and was abandoned by both parents. Her early childhood was spent with her father, who later had to leave her as he was in the military and had to go off to war. Ann was eight when she ran after his car as he drove down the long driveway for the last time. At nine, she learned he was a prisoner of war. She thought she had lost him forever.

Ann was taken into the home of an aunt who lived in the countryside but not taken into the family. Ann was an outsider and treated that way. Her depression grew to the point where she contemplated suicide. She didn't remember many of the details but believed she survived by becoming close to nature. She loved the countryside and fell in love with nature, the beauty of the hills, and the ground itself. It was as if nature nurtured her during these early years.

Feeling abandoned, she attached herself to nature as a source of comfort and strength. She couldn't attach to people because they weren't there for her physically or emotionally. She turned to fantasy when faced with an impossible situation.

She fell in love with Donald in her early twenties, and he became the love of her life. They resonated with each other. She felt abandoned again and thought he had left her when he went off to college in America. She rejected him for leaving and went on with her life. Devastated by her rejection, Donald married another, as did she. However, her love for him never faltered. Even though she was once angry with him for going off to school, her heart was forever enmeshed with his. She described him as her connection to nature.

Ann was seventy when she came to see me for help to cope with cancer and to resolve the lifelong relationship with a man she could never have—a love that would never be fulfilled. Ann believed her body had been weakened by the constant stress of not being able to be with her beloved. Although she was happily married and had a family, she had always held out hope that one day they could be together at last. The stress of holding onto unfulfilled dreams had affected her body, mind, and spirit. We will follow Ann's story, beginning with how her body served her.

Ann had been wiping tears from her eyes. I asked her what she was feeling. She said she was all right and didn't know why her eyes were tearing. I suspected her tears had something to do with the topic of conversation—her coming to realize she was never going to be with Donald in the way she wanted.

Ann began talking about Donald and how she would like to have spent her life with him. I asked if any part of her body was feeling uncomfortable. She immediately motioned to her chest and throat. I asked her to notice what emotion might be associated with the physical discomfort. Without delay, she said there was a part of her afraid of something. She almost cried as she came closer to her feelings. I asked her to go along with my suggestions and see what happens. I brought her to a very relaxed state of mind, and this is what I said:

> Me: Take your awareness, and just sit with the feelings in your chest and throat. Tolerate the discomfort as much as you can. Just notice it. Pay attention to it. See where it takes you. Hear what it has to say. Spend time here. Learn all about what is there. Allow your feelings to guide you. Thank your body and ask what it wants. Ask what it fears. Take all the time you need to be with what is causing this discomfort. When you are done, just bring your awareness back to normal, and we will talk about your experience.

When Ann was finished, she opened her eyes and talked about how the discomfort seemed to melt away. Just sitting with the pain helped her release some of it. She was becoming more in touch with her feelings and learning she was able to survive experiencing her emotions. Ann was on her way to bringing her love for Donald into balance. Her story will be continued in the chapters to come.

CHAPTER 5

Your Conscious Mind

Notice Your Thinking

We have the ability to observe ourselves in action. You have the ability to notice what you notice, ask yourself why you're reacting the way you are, and discover the underlying reason.

Here is an example of what I mean. I like to go fishing early in the morning. This particular morning was special because it was the first time I was fishing from my new boat. The sun had just come up, the air was fresh and cool, and the water was like glass. I had three fishing rods trolling for stripers, and my boat was working perfectly. I was feeling on top of the world.

Then it occurred to me that I hadn't caught a fish. My mood went from being on top of the world to feeling frustrated, and a little stupid for spending all this money on a boat and fishing equipment and having nothing to show for it.

What happened? My emotions reflected my thinking. All I did was have a thought, and my mood immediately shifted to match what I was thinking. I decided to focus on what was right with my world and not judge the day by the number of fish I had caught, or in this situation, not caught.

Being able to notice my thoughts allowed me to change my thinking about catching fish and return to enjoying the moment. I remembered that an emotion always follows a thought, so I could change my emotions by controlling my thoughts. As I sat back and took in a deep breath, I remembered how my father used to grouse about the fish not biting. I had behaved just like my father.

History and Heredity

Whether you knew them or not, parents pass along both their physical and personality traits to their children. Studies of identical twins separated at birth prove heredity plays a major role in how one sees the world, right down to preference for beer and wine. We like to believe we have control over our fundamental behaviors and beliefs, but reams of evidence support the influence of heredity. I call this our internal wiring. Sometimes our internal wiring takes over. No matter what we believe, we can be taken over by influences beyond our control.

Drug and alcohol addiction is a good example. Those with a genetic history that includes drug and alcohol addictions are more susceptible to becoming addicted than those without that genetic history. The same can be true for personality traits. One client noted that his relationship history was just like his mother's— chaotic. Don was addicted to rescuing dysfunctional people and finding himself embroiled in chaos. Looking at his family, Don realized that similar traits filled both sides of his family tree. Was his propensity to be trapped in dysfunctional relationships learned or inherited? Rather than argue the issue, Don realized he was as powerless over saving dysfunctional people as he was powerless over alcohol. The only way to stay out of trouble was to realize he was powerless and to avoid the temptation of rescuing someone.

Positive beliefs can become a buffer against genetic influences. Similarly, negative beliefs, resulting from childhood experiences, can be resolved by replacing them with more appropriate beliefs. The goal of this section is to provide some examples of how heredity and beliefs shape your experience and how these beliefs are formed. You can change by correcting some out-of-date beliefs and negative ways of thinking.

Becoming Conscious

You would be held hostage by your limiting beliefs and genetic influences if you couldn't observe what was causing you to react one way or another. Change any belief that restricts your psychological freedom. Avoid the things you can't control, and change limiting beliefs so you can be free to make any choice you want.

Be as conscious as you can be. The more conscious you are, the more you will be able to notice when your thinking is irrational. Here are some examples.

1. *Labeling* groups everyone together and makes them the villain. Labeling also separates you from those you label. It leads to statements like, "They're ignorant and don't know what they are doing." "They're all idiots." "The army got me again." Instead of labeling, be specific and describe specific behaviors or a particular person. Instead of labeling the army as the villain, name the particular person whose decision or behavior was offensive. Blaming the army makes you powerless while identifying one person puts things into perspective.
2. *Mind reading* assumes you know what a person thinks and why he or she acted one way or another. It leads

to statements like, "They didn't pick me because they always pick one of their own kind." "He said he was sick because he wanted attention." "She did what she did because she knew I would get angry." These mind-reading assumptions reflect the *story* you attach to an event.

3. *Fortune-telling* predicts someone will behave in a certain way. Often, if you predict bad things, it can become a self-fulfilling prophecy. It leads to statements like: "Something always happens to keep me from being a success." "They will never pick me." "They are always going around me to my boss and don't respect me or what I do for the organization." Fortune-telling sets you up for disappointment and doesn't give you the opportunity to see the reality of a situation. Instead, you see a past disappointment being projected onto the future.

4. *Awfulizing* overdramatizes or exaggerates the truth with black-and-white thinking. Everything is negative, with no hope of there being anything good about to happen. It leads to statements like, "I can't stand it." "This company is so messed up. I'll never get recognized and promoted." Awfulizing reflects the feeling that nothing will ever change, time is standing still, and I'm helpless to do anything about it.

5. *Minimizing* distorts reality to fit a negative perception. Your mind doesn't see what is right in the world when it's fixated on all that's wrong. If you believe you are a victim, you will tend to magnify events that support this belief and minimize events that run contrary to being a victim. For example, you forget that you were first in your class and only remember not being picked to play in the band. Distortions take place when you focus on what was unpleasant and forget the good things that happened.

Start noticing your thoughts. Notice if you have any of the above thought patterns. Begin to think about where your beliefs originate and if they need changing. You created your beliefs and the way you think, and you can change what you created.

The Power of a Belief

Remember the story of Jane's surgery? She had married relatively late in life and was an independent-minded, intelligent, and professional success by any definition. Her story started with having minor surgery on her left arm. She described how she had to complete various projects at work before going on vacation. Her niece was with her at work as she typed away on a sales contract. All of a sudden, the incision on her left arm started to bleed. She called her doctor, who advised her to apply direct pressure and elevate her arm to reduce the bleeding. So she did just what the doctor ordered. She held her left arm above her head, asked her niece to apply direct pressure, and continued typing.

What a picture! I stopped her and asked, "What do you think was going on?" I wanted Jane to look at the scene as if it was a metaphor.

> Me: Jane, what's this scene all about?
>
> Jane: I don't know. I had to finish the contract before going on vacation. My clients told me they pushed ahead with their decision to buy, because they knew I was about to leave for a few weeks, and they wanted me to present the contract before I left.
>
> Me: Couldn't you delegate the writing of the contract to one of your staff?

Jane: Well, I could have. I hired a new person who just got laid off because her company reorganized, but I didn't feel comfortable asking her to do what was really my responsibility. I felt funny asking someone who had just been a vice president to do my typing.

Me: Is it hard for you to ask for help?

Jane: Yes, I guess so. I don't really know because I usually do it myself. Who else is going to do it?

Me: What is the source of this belief? Think about this for a minute. Let this situation take you back to your childhood. See if any memories come to mind that reflect similar thinking.

Jane: I recall my mother telling me to take care of my younger sisters. I had two younger sisters, and Mother was always asking me to look after them. There was no one else to do it.

Me: Keep going. What conclusions did you come to? What was the by-product of those experiences?

Jane: I learned that I was number three after my two younger sisters. I never thought of it before, and I know it's not true. My mother had five kids. She couldn't do it all by herself, so she needed help from the older kids. She didn't think of me as being less important. She just needed my help.

I seem to put others ahead of me. I always have difficulty asking for help. I guess I don't want to make them feel the way I felt when my mother interrupted what I was doing to ask me to help her. I thought what I was doing wasn't important, and my younger sisters were more important.

Me: What's the truth?

Jane: Well, I know I'm as important as anyone else.

Me: Yes, I'm sure you believe you are as important as anyone else. That's common sense. Nevertheless, do you ever find yourself being victimized by the needs of others?

Jane: Yes, and I get angry with them and myself.

Me: Give me an example of how you get angry when someone's needs make you feel you aren't important.

Jane: When my husband does it, I make sure I schedule events so he will be late. He hates being late.

Me: So you are passive-aggressive? [With that, her face is flushed, her jaw tenses, and I think she is angry with me.]

Jane: Passive-aggressive! I don't like that idea. That's not me.

Me: I think you felt like a victim when his needs were more important than yours—just as it was when your sisters' needs were more important than yours. To correct this imbalance, you victimized him, but in a sophisticated way of *getting even*. Please realize your passive-aggressive response was not planned. It was an automatic response to your underlying belief that your needs aren't important—hence you aren't important. And that idea made you angry.

Jane: I think that's true. There are more situations when I came second, third, or whatever. Now that I look at why I was typing a contract with one hand while holding my bleeding arm above my head, it was because my client's needs came first, money came second, and I was third.

Me: If a client or money are things you choose to put ahead of your needs, you might want to make yourself third again. But at least you will be making a conscious choice and not feel like a victim. Looking back, what would you have done differently?

Jane: I would have asked my staff to write the contract and not over functioned like I usually do.

Within a month she was asking others for help. Change usually takes some time and can be hard when it involves others. You must go through the process of unlearning a behavior. You have to force yourself to act differently. I don't want anyone to think this stuff is easy. It isn't.

Changing automatic behaviors that are learned in early childhood are difficult, because they have been your *normal* for so many years. Children come to conclusions about themselves and others as a consequence of normal family activities. There was no abuse, no yelling, and no physical abuse. Jane simply came to the conclusion that others were more important. After all, don't good people put others ahead of themselves?

Let's look at the power of learned values. Jane's mother and grandmother were taught how to be good women. But women who were raised by the standards of the thirties, forties, and fifties are going to be plowed under in today's corporate world. Good women in her mother's time were taught their husbands, children, and friends came first. Putting others ahead of yourself will not serve you if you are running a business or making policy decisions for a major corporation.

Jane's story illustrates how powerful your mind can be and how beliefs influence concepts of yourself and others. Beliefs are the source of your thinking, and they provide the structure of your world. You must have beliefs to give structure to your life. Beliefs provide the illusion of order that is necessary to function. It's your way of understanding the present and predicting the future. Beliefs are necessary. Your job is to make them conscious and to reflect reality.

CHAPTER 6

Your Unconscious Mind

Definitions

Let's begin with some history and a few definitions.

According to my dictionary, the *unconscious* is defined as the part of the mind below the level of conscious. In psychoanalytic theory, *unconscious* is defined as the division of the mind that contains the elements of your psychic makeup—such as memories or repressed desires—that are not subject to conscious perception or control but that often affect conscious thoughts and behavior.

To provide just a bit more clarity, I use *unconscious mind* when referring to the container holding and managing *unconscious* material. I see the unconscious mind as the place that holds all your unconscious memories, beliefs, thoughts, and conflicts. The unconscious also comprises the soul with the imprint for this life.

You can thank Freud and Jung for developing the theories in use today. Freud believed in psychic determinism—in the power of the unconscious and the strength of instincts. He thought nothing occurred by chance. All behavior was motivated by unconscious conflicts stemming from early childhood and centered on the expression of aggressive and sexual instincts.

According to Jung's theory, you not only have a personal unconscious dealing with your personal history of being a victim or a victimizer, but you also have to integrate your role in the *collective unconscious.* How many times throughout your life have you taken on the role of victim? How many times have you been in the role of victimizer? Both these experiences and associated energetic patterns are within your spirit energy field. Your goal is to evolve to where you are neither victim nor victimizer.

Accept all you have been and done. Hold all aspects of yourself in total understanding and acceptance. See that power and control are no longer the central activity of your relationships. Become secure enough so that you no longer have to prove anything or control anyone. You just are, and you are enough.

When the Old West gunfighter no longer had to prove anything, he took off his guns and put them in his trunk, along with the trappings of the gunfighter. He had passed through that phase of his life and moved on. He no longer needed a gunfighter identity. Yet, when necessary, he could open his old trunk, pull out his six-guns, and deal with the bad guys.

Jung added to Freud's concept of the *personal* unconscious by connecting us to the *collective* human experience. The collective unconscious was Jung's term for memory traces that he believed are shared by the human race, regardless of when you lived or will live.

Jung felt that neither the personal nor the collective unconscious could be contacted directly. So he developed several methods that tapped what he believed to be rich sources of potential for growth. The creative techniques Jungians use to elicit unconscious material include reading and writing, poetry, drawing, modeling in clay, discussing daydreams, fantasies, and "ideas out of the blue," and most importantly, nocturnal dreams. These activities all suspend the conscious mind's control that allows the unconscious to take over. The unconscious is then able to create the image or trigger an intuitive moment or a thought out of the blue. You have been using imagery to help your conscious mind relax and watch what your unconscious produces.

Unconscious Functions

Think of your unconscious as performing many functions that are designed to protect and serve your conscious mind. Your unconscious is the container for old memories you don't need cluttering your day-to-day life. Imagine what it would be like to remember absolutely everything that ever happened. Who wants to remember what they had for breakfast ten years ago? Theoretically, what you had for breakfast ten years ago is filed away somewhere, or maybe it isn't. It really doesn't matter. What matters is that an event that hurt you in the past is still part of your unconscious memory today and may be the source of a negative belief that is overly influencing your daily life.

Your unconscious manages any particular event by assigning some amount of psychic energy to serve as a container for the unconscious material. The unconscious material is stored in the form of images and emotions, so the material you get back may only be a symbolic representation of the actual event. Jung paid attention to dreams, fantasies, and poetic writing —all manifestations coming out of a dream-state where the conscious mind is suspended enough to observe the unconscious material.

Influencing the Unconscious

The unconscious is influenced by childhood experiences. Freud focused on desires, conflicts, and sex. But many other issues—acceptance, rejection, trust, and mistrust—have to be considered. Adolescents want to be accepted by their peer group. This results in peer group pressure. Kids will do just about anything to be accepted by those who are important to them.

You start life needing to be accepted by your parents, but in adolescence, your needs shift from parents to same-gender friends. Body size, looking good, being like the other kids, and being part of a social scene become very important. During these times, you experience either being part of the group or being on the outside looking in.

After adolescence, you look to the work world to determine whether you are a success or a failure. If you had a positive experience as a child and were able to belong to a peer group, you probably internalized a sense that you are okay. You are able to fall back on a positive internalized idea of yourself. If you didn't have a positive childhood experience, you might find yourself looking outside of yourself to find acceptance and self-worth. This can be dangerous. It means you give up your personal power.

Your unconscious contains an imprint, or energetic impression, of your life, along with a projection of who you are now and who you will be in the future. You are influenced by, and live *through,* past experiences that significantly influence both your worldview and personal view. You see this in action by the way you relate to others. How you relate to authority figures is influenced by your relationship with your parents. How you relate to friends is influenced by how you related to your peer group. To resolve the negative impact of your early experiences, you must go to where the damage took place and revisit these early experiences to gain understanding, find acceptance, and create an appropriate belief.

Changing any aspect of your internal projection requires that you to delve into your unconscious material to bring it into your conscious mind. This is part of creating a union between your unconscious and conscious self. Traumatic memories, negative beliefs, and unconscious fears may be restricting your free will and free choice. You can't evolve if you are afraid to take risks. Remember, your purpose is to live the experiences that life offers.

You may have heard the phrase *healing the child within.* You must work on your inner children, as well as issues already present at your birth. Some people are comfortable with the concept of another life, while others may not be, but it really doesn't matter whether one believes in other lives or not. What matters is what you are holding in your spirit. The source of the victim energy may be in this life or another life, or it may be an attachment to someone you know who has been victimized. Again, it really doesn't matter. What matters is finding a way to resolve what isn't working. I approach what isn't working like a car mechanic approaches a car engine that won't start. I know the theory of how engines run and what is necessary to start a car. With my theory in hand, I start through the steps to discover what isn't working. Without first having a theory, I wouldn't know where to begin.

Theories regarding how life works are useful because they provide a *story* that fills the void created by not knowing. Nature hates a vacuum. We hate a vacuum, so we create a theory that serves as a placeholder until a better theory comes along. I learned I had to bring my mind along as I searched for the answers to why I'm here. I found having a theory provided my mind a structure that would make sense out of what I was experiencing.

The theories I had growing up gave way to theories I developed as a young adult, and those continued to evolve as I grew older. Always searching, always wanting to know how it all worked was forever with me. Now I understand my searching was part of my unconscious blueprint. I'm like a prospector searching for gold so he can become rich and share all he has with everyone.

While understanding a theory is nice, it's of little value unless one can accomplish something with it. I've learned that while my mind may *want* to know, what is most important is finding the way for a person's unconscious to resolve what needs fixing. *Knowing* isn't required. In fact, *not* knowing is the first step in communicating with the unconscious. The next step is to ask questions. Remember, your unconscious is all knowing. That doesn't mean it will answer every question. It won't. Most answers will come through an experience.

When your mind thinks it knows something, it doesn't listen, and there is no communication with your unconscious. Getting comfortable with not knowing, and asking for guidance from within, is essential for internal communication.

The method for communicating with the unconscious varies with each person. Some people are visual and picture things in their imagination. For others who may just sense or feel a response, it is a difficult task for them to picture an object in their mind's eye. Others who are neither visual nor feeling may think their way along. For them, I suggest they look for an inspired thought that seems to come out of the blue—a thought they didn't consciously create.

CHAPTER 7

Healing Your Spirit

The first thing one does in preparation for a journey is to make one's vessel seaworthy. You begin by working on yourself to resolve anything that might limit your ability to endure hardships along the way. You want to be of sound mind, body, and spirit.

When I speak of spirit, I refer to the energy associated with your personality. If you were traumatized as a child, your personality may have split up, with each small segment taking away its part of your spirit energy. Your goal is to bring together all of your spirit energy, so your soul and spirit can come together.

In my work as a mental health therapist in a county jail, I had the opportunity to help some very wounded clients. It was in the jail that I encountered my first client with multiple personalities and realized I needed specialized training and supervision. Statistically, 1 percent of the general population has been diagnosed with dissociative identity disorder (DID), which used to be called multiple personality disorder (MPD). I believe there are many people with undiagnosed DID because the symptoms are misdiagnosed as schizophrenia or bipolar disorder.

Among the books I have read on the treatment of multiple personality disorder was one by Dr. Ralph B. Allison, MD, who described discovering what he called an inside spiritual helper (ISH) among the client's dissociated parts. Fascinated by his description, I began to include his suggestion to seek the help of an ISH. These spiritual helpers have been known to help the therapist organize and carry out a treatment plan.

Not all my clients with multiple personalities had an ISH, but a few did. Their assistance ran the spectrum from a little help to very helpful. They helped me understand the spiritual aspect of treatment. The following is an excerpt from my case notes of October 12, 1998:

> This client has six personalities, each with their own set of emotions. I asked the ISH if she could help me understand how the client's personality system was organized. The ISH provided a new way of thinking about the relationships between the mind, spirit, body, heart, and soul. The ISH described how the spirit and mind work together at one level, as the heart and soul work at another. She described the body as the temple, containing the DNA memory imprinted by the soul upon entering the flesh. The soul is connected to the universe and guides the spirit in becoming whole so both can return to the Creator. The following was the message from the spirit helper:

1. Emotions have split up the spirit (referring to the client).
2. When tormented too much, the spirit cannot be "picked up" at the death of the body.
3. The soul belongs to the Creator.
4. Spirit can linger behind when it is not whole.
5. One's spirit and soul have to be one to go on to the Creator.

6. The soul is associated with the heart. Spirit is associated with the mind.
7. When not intact, the soul is in danger of losing the spirit and remains in a paradox between heaven and earth.
8. The body is the temple that contains both soul and spirit.
9. When the spirit is healed, or made one, it joins the soul.
10. Emotions cause the spirit to split up.

In applying what the ISH said, the mind splits into various fragments in response to overwhelming emotions. As the mind splits, so too does the spirit split into segments that remain associated with the segments of mind or personality. Healing occurs when the mind and spirit energies come together, so that the mind/spirit is intact with soul/heart. The treatment goal is to bring all the parts back together, along with all of their segmented parts of spirit that have suffered fragmentation over the eons.

An Angel at the Table

I was treating a client, Lynn, who had multiple personalities—a male protector part, several children, and one older child. As a survivor of childhood sexual abuse, she had split off parts of her personality to survive.

This wasn't the first time one of my clients reported seeing an angelic figure, but somehow this was different. Lynn had been in therapy before and had done a lot of work. We had been working for several months to get the entire inside family together around an inside meeting table. She knew who the players were and their functions within the personality system. It had taken some doing to coax all of her alters to sit together. There was mistrust between some of the adults, and the children were afraid of one of the male alters.

This was the fourth in a series of inside meetings in which positive memories were being shared. They were getting really good at it. Memories could be packaged into a softball-sized ball of light and tossed to one another. If all wanted to participate, the energy could be sent around the circle, and each would "get" the memory of the sender. They had just finished sharing an early school memory when Lynn noted that it was the anniversary of the death of her father.

Lynn had mixed feelings about her father, so I asked if anyone at the table would object to my asking each to express how they felt about this day being the anniversary of his death. I thought it would be an opportunity for me to find out how they had arranged themselves around the table.

One by one, each expressed their thoughts or feelings. I would ask Lynn, who was serving as moderator, who among the group was next to share. When we reached the end of my list of known alters, I asked who was next.

Lynn looked puzzled for a moment. "There is an empty chair at the table."

She said she couldn't see anyone sitting in the chair and didn't think anyone was missing. I asked if anyone at the table could see who was sitting in the chair. One of the children said it was where the angel sat.

"Really," I said in the most matter-of-fact way I could muster. "I wonder if the angel would be willing to join us at the table."

The child reported that it would take a few moments for the angel Annette to come. I asked all the parts to hold hands and adjust to the frequency of the child alter who could begin to see Annette's arrival. As she became visible to the group, there was a mixed response. Some were surprised. Others thought this all was nuts while saying it was "cool." With Annette fully visible to the group, I welcomed her.

"Thank you for coming," I said to her, all the while thinking as fast as I could what to do next.

Sometimes I take on too much responsibly and think I have to always know what to do. While I was thinking too much, one of the alters asked Annette a question. "Why didn't you protect me from the abuse?"

Lynn reported that Annette didn't talk, but all could hear her thoughts. Annette responded, "I couldn't protect you from harm, but I can help you all through life's events." Someone asked where Annette came from, if she had been in a body before.

Annette said, "I just am."

I asked Annette a question. "Would you be willing to send your energy around the circle?"

She agreed, and we sat in silence until Lynn once again opened her eyes and spoke. "It feels warm." The look on Lynn's face said more than her words. They could feel the energy.

Time was up, and we brought the session to a close. All the alters left the meeting room. Annette went back to where angels wait and watch. I pondered the experience and was left with my own thoughts and feelings. Should I just file this one away as a client's vivid imagination, or should I accept the possibility that it was what it was?

Experiences outside of your normal are labeled as strange or unusual. You make up a story to explain what you experienced and isolate it in a file with other unexplainable experiences. Your life continues as if nothing had happened, so nothing changes. This is how you avoid change. You simply dismiss the experience.

The bad news: if you dismiss enough experiences, you end up dismissing the opportunity to fulfill your life's purpose. You waste a lifetime. The good news: you have free will and free choice. You can choose to make life a spiritual journey.

Heal Yourself

You may have had to split off parts of your personality to cope with whatever was happening to you. Your mind and spirit may have had to divide to survive. Understand that splitting up was necessary, and it is now time to come back together. I know you can bring your parts back together and heal because I have helped many clients do it. Now I'm sharing what I learned. Let's begin with what you have been taught.

You have been *domesticated* to fit into society. You were taught what to do, what not to do, what to believe, what not to believe. To question was often if not always a dangerous undertaking. I don't know about you, but questioning authority has gotten me in trouble a few times.

It's not that parents and teachers were purposely doing a job on you. They were passing along what they had learned, in most cases doing the best they could. You watched, listened, and developed your beliefs from your childhood experiences. When you were hurt, Mom took care of you. You were little boys and girls in a big world and looked to others for comfort and healing. You learned that others had the power to heal. What you didn't learn was that you could heal yourself.

Part of creating a new normal is breaking out of your personal prison. You live within a cellblock of limiting beliefs that are guarded by fear. Your *body, mind,* and *spirit* are held captive by your past. Let's start by looking at how each of these primary elements can be made whole again.

Body

Healing your *body* refers to eliminating symptoms caused either by emotional issues or past events that have been caught and stored within the fabric of your physiology. Your body stores unfinished emotional and physical trauma. If you are unable to digest an event, the event gets stored in your body, where it can convert into a physical problem.

Mind

Because you are aware of your thoughts, dealing with your *conscious mind* is straightforward. You know what you believe and don't believe. You are able to check on any irrational thinking and limiting beliefs that shape your outlook and contribute to negative outcomes. What you *think* has a lot to do with how you *feel* and what you believe you can or cannot do. If you believe that you will end up alone and a bag lady, I suggest you change your belief.

The contents of your *unconscious mind* are unseen and mostly unknown. If your mind were the ocean, your conscious mind would be from the surface down to the depth you could dive. Your unconscious mind would extend into the abyss, where the gold is located, carefully guarded by underwater dragons. Your challenge is to enter the abyss, slay the dragons, and get the gold.

The dragons, of course, are your fears. The gold is to achieve psychological freedom.

Spirit

Your soul is like a diamond—everlasting. It cannot be fragmented. But your spirit is like soft coal that can be fragmented and must be brought into wholeness with your soul.

The goal is to become whole in body, mind, and spirit to empower you with free will and free choice. You can achieve this goal by working to free your body of unprocessed trauma; conscious and unconscious mind of repressed emotions, experiences, and irrational beliefs, and bring together its fragmented parts; and spirit from unhealthy attachments to others and to bring back its fragmented parts.

CHAPTER 8

Attachments

About Thoughts

Let's start by thinking about thoughts. We don't think about thought very much. We just think our thoughts, and that's about it. Most of our thinking is automatic. We don't spend a lot of time noticing what we are thinking, let alone what the impact of our thoughts is.

We know emotion always follows thought. We think of a sad situation and find ourselves feeling sad. None of this is new. So let's look at a thought as a form of energy that radiates out from the thinker. Each thought is energy that is being transmitted much like a radio wave.

Transmitting Energy

When you think, you transmit energy. In fact, you can actually think yourself right out of your body. This concept isn't new, by any means. People have been thinking themselves out of their bodies for lots of reasons.

The stories in this chapter will focus on the spiritual aspects of life and how you can heal yourself by working with your unconscious. You are always transmitting and receiving spirit energy. Some people can walk into a room full of people and feel that something is wrong.

The energy is the spirit of those in the room—the personalities present. You can experience the energy of others, and they can experience yours. You can also find yourself attached to others as they can attach to you. The most common attachments are with your family members. Some are positive, and others are negative.

Identifying Negative Attachment

Kim was a thirty-year-old professional woman who seemed to have everything, but she was in turmoil. The following exchange illustrates the impact of attachments:

> Me: I notice you're very uncomfortable right now. What are you thinking about?
>
> Kim: My father asked me what my next project was going to be. I always feel inadequate when he asks me questions like that.
>
> Me: Where in your body do you feel this discomfort?
>
> Kim: I feel it in my stomach.
>
> Me: I'd like you to use your imagination to go inside your stomach and meet the part that is feeling so bad. When you have a good connection with her, ask what's causing her to feel so bad.
>
> Kim: She feels bad because her father isn't happy with her, and she wants her father to love her.

Me: Of course she does. She is very attached to her father. Ask her if she needs him.

Kim: Yes, very much. She is attached to him and needs his acceptance, but she believes she isn't good enough.

Me: Find the perfect way that will allow her to detach from her father. I know you don't know how right now, so go ahead and ask your unconscious. I'm sure an idea will pop into your head. Take all the time you want to ask for the perfect way for her to detach from her father.

Kim: I took her up in my arms and loved her myself. I then asked her to experience how much she was loved and accepted by my heart, to notice that I'm an adult and old enough for her to be my child. A mirror appeared, and we stood next to each other. As soon as she saw our reflections, she laughed and went away to play.

Me: Is the attachment to your father broken?

Kim: Yes, it broke when she and I realized that we no longer need his approval and that his concerns about money and prestige were all about him and his fears and not about me.

Me: Well done! Excellent work.

This story illustrates how attachments can overly influence your mood, let alone your life. The attachment was created out of a need to be loved and the belief that her father didn't love her. The belief created an attachment between father and daughter. It's as if the spirit of the daughter meshed with her father's spirit.

During the weeks that followed, Kim noticed how she was more relaxed around her father and how she felt more like an adult around him instead of a child. She successfully adjusted her belief about her father, integrated the child within, and resolved the associated energetic (spirit) attachment.

Detaching from Others—Ann's Story (Continued)

Earlier I introduced you to Ann, who was born in England before World War II and was abandoned by both of her parents. She was attached to Donald, the love of her life.

Ann's story provides a good example of a dysfunctional attachment that prevented her from moving beyond her childhood abandonment. When Ann met Donald, he filled a great need in her, just as she filled a great need in him. Once they were attached, their relationship remained the same for decades. She was safe as long as she was attached to Donald. Separating meant she had to become emotionally independent.

Ann was ready to make the transition from *needing* Donald to simply enjoying his friendship. She had given him her heart in return for the promise of undying love. But now she agreed that she had been too attached to him and was ready to detach. It was time to take back what was hers. Would taking back her heart mean she must stop loving him?

You can love someone without an attachment so strong that it fragments your spirit. Loving from your wholeness creates a connection that is freely offered. The *need* for love to be secure is replaced by a sharing of two hearts from a place of fullness. When love fills a void, you become dependent—a slave to the relationship like Ann was a slave to Donald. It was time to heal Ann's childhood wounds so she could be free to evolve the relationship.

It wasn't easy. It took many sessions to heal enough where Ann was willing to change her relationship with Donald. Their relationship started with a thought that was created from the belief that she needed him to survive. Since it was a thought that started the relationship, only a thought was required to end it. The old relationship had to end for a new one to be created.

While some people require a ritual or structured process to detach, Ann simply decided to take back her spirit, and that's what happened. She sat in silence for a few minutes. "I felt something come into my chest," she said. No bells or whistles—just a quiet transition.

A week later, Ann received a letter from Donald. She wrote a response back to him, as she would with any friend. She said she felt differently toward him. While the romantic fantasy born in her youth was gone, there was a new relationship that was even better. It was real. Ann had done the work required to eliminate the need for fantasy.

Detaching Others from You

I'll bet someone is attached to you. Spirit attachments work both ways. You attach to others, and others attach to you. These attachments are often welcome and reciprocal. They satisfy needs. Sometimes, however, they can become a burden.

Relationships sometimes serve their purpose and then come to an end. It's great when both parties agree to terminate a relationship and move on with their lives. But what happens when someone can't or won't detach? How do you tell if someone is attached to you? The technique I suggest is to acknowledge that you don't know if someone has attached to you and to ask your unconscious.

You have to rely on communication between your conscious and your unconscious. Your conscious mind is not designed to know about spirit attachments beyond the intellectual understanding. Your unconscious has access to all the information you need. All you have to do is ask, and the answer is immediate. The following is a typical example.

Betty had recently divorced her husband. She had been very much in love with him, and that made the separation and divorce difficult. She was now dating and moving in a new circle of friends, but her ex-husband continued to occupy space in her head. Was Betty still attached to him? Was he still attached to her?

The answer to both of these questions was a strong yes. There were parts of Betty that still needed to be attached. Her husband had made her feel important, loved, and taken care of. The needy parts of Betty were reluctant to let go and detach from her husband, who provided a way to leave home and start her own family. Once Betty discovered she was strong enough to go on without her ex-husband, it was time for her to take back her spirit and send his spirit back to him. They were both attached to each other. How could we tell? We asked her unconscious.

Letting Go

I asked Betty to imagine a TV screen. I spoke quietly in a monotone voice as she moved into a relaxed state of mind. We had done this before, and Betty was willing to do her work. After only a few seconds, she said she had her TV set in front of her. I suggested she simply ask her unconscious to project the word *yes* onto her inside TV if there was spirit energy from her ex-husband still attached to her.

"His spirit is attached to me," she said. I asked if she was willing to send what was his back to him. "Yes," she said. "I'm ready."

It was important to get permission from all aspects of Betty. Parts of the personality are often reluctant to let go. We had spent several sessions getting ready for this day. She was definitely ready. I suggested we not send him away with negative thoughts. We wanted to send him away with neutral intentions, recognizing that it was right that each had their spirit free from the other.

The next step was to create a structured way to facilitate the transfer of spirit. Since Betty liked animals, I asked that a picture of an animal be projected onto her inside TV screen. I wanted her unconscious to select the perfect animal to make the transfer of spirit. I suggested the perfect animal be projected onto her screen at the count of three. At the count of three, a picture of a dolphin was projected onto the screen. I then asked Betty to make sure that the dolphin was willing to take her ex-husband's spirit back to him. I told Betty her dolphin could talk and to just ask it any question she wanted to ask. Of course, you know the dolphin was simply a projection from her unconscious, so of course it could talk. It could do anything she wanted it to do.

The dolphin agreed to take her ex-husband's spirit back to him and began to move all through Betty, collecting his spirit. When the dolphin left her, she reported feeling much lighter. We used a similar technique to bring back her spirit from him.

Betty's goals were accomplished. She was ready to be free. The method we used to accomplish the transfer of spirit was not as important as her willingness to detach and bring back what was hers. Nothing could happen without her being clear about what she wanted.

Detaching from Mother

Every time Dean was around women, he felt like an insecure child. He was twenty-five and searching for a reason why he was afraid of women.

Our first step was to find out what was causing his discomfort.

We used an inside meeting room to call in the part that was afraid. He went into his imagination and soon was describing himself around the age of eight. He learned he was very afraid of his mother. He never felt he pleased her and began to believe he was somehow lacking. This caused him to believe women would not accept him and would find him inadequate. The eight-year-old part was attached to his mother and still trying to obtain her love and acceptance. When confronted with a female relationship, the eight-year-old part would emerge and overly influence Dean's thoughts and feelings.

We used the following technique to detach Dean from his mother.

> Me: Dean, go ahead and tell the eight-year-old the truth. He is stuck in time and continues to seek his mother's approval. Introduce him to the present time and to you as a mature man.
>
> Dean: He knows the truth now. That's funny. Once he realized he was really all right, he changed his entire attitude. The whole thing is funny.
>
> Me: Good job. I take it that the young part is now free from his fearful attachment to Mom.
>
> Dean: Yes, definitely.

Dean was able to feel the difference. His young part came together with the rest of Dean once it knew the truth about his mother's behavior and his need for approval. Fear of women was no longer necessary.

This technique is a simple way to resolve attachments. You simply find the part that is attached, find out why it's attached, and change the underlying belief. Often there is a fear-based belief at the root of a negative attachment that was formed by a child.

Security and love are frequently the underlying issues that cause you to form attachments. While it's nice to be connected with those who provide feelings of security and love, it isn't fair to them or you to be too dependent on them.

CHAPTER 9

Spirit Realm

As you have moved through this book, you have been moving from one aspect of yourself to another. You visited your body, then your conscious mind, followed by your unconscious mind. Now is the time to visit your spirit. Your goal is to become aware of what needs attention so you are able to fulfill your purpose and create your new normal.

This chapter will address energetic wounds and how to heal them. Your spirit is your energetic body. It's you as a spiritual being moving from life to life on a journey filled with all the *experiences* needed to accomplish your soul's purpose. Some of these experiences can tear you down mentally, physically, and spiritually. The process of being torn down and rebuilding seems to be part of the evolutionary process. As they say, "What doesn't kill you makes you stronger." For those with a multi-life perspective, what does kill them also makes them strong.

Healing a Fragmented Spirit

Fragmentation is simply a situation where part of your spirit is no longer with you. It was given away, taken, or split off during an experience that was so strong it resulted in your spirit being fragmented. Some of your spirit stayed behind while the rest of you moved on. Essentially, you split up your spirit to cope with an experience that was too painful to contain at the time. Life experiences afford you the opportunity to heal unresolved spiritual wounds that are brought into this life. Spiritual wounds move from life to life until they are resolved.

Fragmentation

You have learned how multiple personalities are created. At the spiritual level, the spirit does the same thing, though at a different level. Instead of splitting off parts to cope with a situation in childhood, the spirit can split off to cope with an entire life or a death.

Most people come to therapy to get help for a here-and-now problem. Therapy begins with looking back to see if your immediate problem is part of a pattern of events that point to a deeper issue. Difficult situations may be intended to provide you with the experience you need to move along your journey. When you don't get the message, you can find yourself in a pattern of similar experiences. When this happens, ask your unconscious if you came into this life with the problem. If you get a yes response, ask if you have permission to go back in time to visit the problem's source. If permission is granted, the rest is relatively easy, because your unconscious is already set up to provide the corrective experience.

The following story is an example of unfinished business from a previous life being brought into this one.

Kevin the Betrayed

Kevin reported a pattern of being betrayed. He told story after story of how people took advantage of him. His boss at work took credit for his accomplishments. Friends took him for granted. Girlfriends replaced him.

We looked at his past to find the source of his problem, without success. As a last resort, I asked his unconscious if he had come into this life with the betrayal issue. Bingo—he came in with it.

When we discovered he brought the issue into this life, we went back through several lives and found repeated instances when he had been betrayed and killed. But Kevin was unable to discover the underlying cause. He seemed to be resisting his participation in the betrayal scenario.

Being ready to know the truth is essential to healing. Even though Kevin thought he was ready to resolve the source of his wounding, some part of him resisted. We had to find the part that was protecting Kevin from his past and release it from its gatekeeping responsibilities. We were able to continue once that piece of work was done.

In one of his past lives, he was a leader of a group and enthusiastically ruled and did what he thought was right. Yet he was betrayed and killed by several of his closest friends. Traumatized by the betrayal, the wounded spirit energy came into this life still needing resolution.

Suddenly, he got it. He had been concerned with accomplishing his well-intended goals but didn't see or consider the needs of those around him. He expected everyone to have his point of view.

Traditional therapy wasn't going to get at this kind of problem because it typically doesn't explore other lives to find a spirit wound. The wound was held in a fragmented part of his spirit. Once we found the source of the betrayal issue, Kevin was able to resolve the trauma from another lifetime.

Norma the Rescuer

Recognizing that she was attracted to men who needed rescuing, Norma wanted to work on her relationship patterns. She was married to a man she rescued from a bad marriage and then found herself in a dysfunctional relationship very similar to previously failed relationships. Her husband was controlling her. No matter what she did to please him, she seemed to fail. When we followed the trail back to the source of her relationship pattern, we discovered that she came into this life with an unresolved issue.

She asked her unconscious to go to the source of her need to rescue people. She went back to a life where she saw herself running down the beach after her older brother. He had run into the ocean and seemed to be drowning. Without thinking, in an effort to save him, she ran into the ocean after him. He was too far out, and they both drowned. When she left her body, she felt very bad. She was sure it was her fault that he had died. She was so upset that her spirit split off a part that held her guilt over not being a good sister.

Since brother and sister died at about the same time, I asked the client to go to her brother and ask what happened from his point of view. He said he liked to tease his little sister, who always followed him around. He would play tricks on her, but she was too stupid to see what he was doing. He ran into the ocean to play a trick on her. He knew she couldn't swim and would follow him anyway. He liked to have power over his sister, even though this time things didn't turn out the way he intended.

In this life, she was married to her brother. He was still exercising power over her, and she was still coming to his rescue to earn his love. I suggested she go to the scene where she was running after him, but this time I suggested her spirit show her a different outcome. Once again, she saw herself running down the beach after her brother, who kept running right into the ocean. This time she stopped at the water's edge and yelled to him, "I can't swim." With the game over, he lost interest and struggled back to the beach, arriving exhausted and scared. She had saved him by not saving him. She learned her life was as important as his, and all she had to do was be honest. This wisdom made the integration of her spirit easy. There was no longer any need to rescue either him or anyone else.

All of these stories deal with time, because the wounds happened in the past. When trauma happens in your life as an adult, you deal with it using an adult mind. When trauma happens when you are young, or in another life, you have to go back to the place where the trauma happened. Since we can imagine going back in time, we can also imagine going ahead in time.

Time Travel–Looking Ahead

Looking ahead in time is done in much the same way as looking back. In this next story, Don was at a transition in his life, having trouble deciding what course to take. He didn't want to make a mistake. He asked for some decision-making help.

Don started by talking about his indecision on whether to return to his home in England or remain in the States for an extended period. He talked about his friend John, who seemed to want him around, but only at John's convenience—not too close, but close enough to be there when needed. Don was concerned about his company and those who needed him to be there to make sound decisions. He wanted to do what was right, but right seemed to mean meeting others' expectations at the expense of his own. He thought looking ahead would help him make the right decision. I suggested we check in with his unconscious and see whether looking ahead would be helpful.

We used a TV screen to communicate with Don's unconscious, and he obtained permission to travel into his future. An angelic bubble was created for him to travel to a future time selected by his unconscious. A very large bubble became present. He got in and made himself comfortable, and a beam of light appeared above the bubble. The bubble ascended into the beam, which began to move through time.

The first place the bubble visited was a library with a research center. Don asked what decisions he had made to accomplish this future, and he learned he had to be specific about what he wanted and also to remain focused on his goals.

He wasn't finished, and the bubble moved to another possible future that was located in the country. He found himself at a healing center specializing in herbs. He asked what decisions were made to create this future, and he was told he had followed his instincts. He was still not done and moved to a third possible future that included a school and a research center. Again, he asked what decisions he made to accomplish this future. He was told he got out of his own way, and it all just happened.

When he returned to normal consciousness, I asked what he learned from the experience. He said what stuck in his mind was what he did to accomplish each of the possible futures. He learned to stay focused on his goals, follow his instincts, and get out of his own way. Getting out of his own way was the first thing he needed to do. Fears of rejection and loss were overinfluencing his decisions. He began working on reducing his fears. Within five years, he was well on his way to accomplishing one of the futures presented during this session.

CHAPTER 10

The New You

There are consequences associated with change and creating a new normal. Some friends may drift away. You may notice that you're just not the same as you once were. You've changed somehow, and your friends haven't. You may think they don't like you anymore for some reason. You may find yourself looking for what you must have done or said. You may find you just don't have anything in common anymore. It's okay. It happens when you create a new normal. You are no longer who you were. Your friends notice the change. Your friends want you to stay the same; however, once you evolve, you can't go back. There is only forward.

If you have decided to take life's journey, you are going to find yourself among other seekers who have left their original flock to seek the company of others like them. Those who are content with the group they are in will evolve as the group evolves. If you want to evolve faster than your current group, you must change groups. If you want to grow at your own pace, find people like you who are interested in life as a spiritual journey. You will fly with birds of a feather in a new flock.

The new you will notice people relating to you differently. I think this might be because your energy is different from most people. For example, I was sitting in the waiting area of Bethesda Naval Hospital waiting for my turn to fill some prescriptions. I had an hour to wait, so I found a seat between two people who were passing the time by reading and working a crossword puzzle. I busied myself without interrupting those who were sitting next to me. After fifteen minutes or so, the person on my left got up, and someone else sat down. This person's energy was noticeably different. I actually felt the energy change.

Within two minutes, she began to tell me her story. I learned about her grandmother and how she had to take over from her mother and start the process of getting the grandmother into assisted living. I learned about her husband, a retired air force pilot, who didn't want to tell anyone he needed a kidney transplant. I learned about her unexpressed anger and frustration and secrets untold to friends or family.

She was upset with her husband for telling her to keep his need for a kidney a secret because *he* wasn't ready to talk about it. She had to talk about it, so she told her sister, whom she swore to secrecy. I had explained to her that men often go into their private cave to work through problems on their own. Pilots are particularly sensitive to any situation that might make them vulnerable. You are taught early on to solve your own problems and always be strong. Needing anything is a sign of weakness. Weakness is unacceptable. I helped her understand that he was afraid and not able to show his fear. Once she understood, our conversation was over. Her number came up on the screen, and she left without looking back.

I believe we met for a reason. The lady needed to talk. I must have felt safe to her. I really don't know. I know I have observed people were relating to me differently after I did my healing work and became a little more conscious.

The new you will be more conscious. You will be more aware

of your surroundings. Opportunities will come your way, and people will find you as you find them. It's like being at a dance. If you stand against the wall and hope someone will find you, your chances of being noticed are very limited. If you get out onto the dance floor and move with the music, putting your energy into the dance, you will be noticed.

The universe can only respond to the energy you give out.

Coming Together

Your goal in creating a new normal is to come together. You started by recognizing your body and how it was holding past experiences that you split off. You looked into your conscious and your unconscious to bring together split-off parts. You ended up looking into your spiritual energy to bring together its fragmented parts.

Once you brought yourself together energetically, you were able to begin connecting to others. Eventually you recognized that we are all connected. When that happened, you recognized we are all one, and all will eventually come together.

The Need to Surrender

As you proceed along your journey, you will notice how much you have surrendered. You will have surrendered your need to worry about the past. You will not worry about things you cannot control. You will notice you have willingly surrendered to the synchronicity that guides your life.

Desire creates synchronicity. The universe is designed to fulfill your deepest desires, hence the age old adage, "Be careful what you ask for." A desire to be in a loving relationship is better than a desire to be with a rich, five-foot-three, single (choose a color) female who will fulfill your every dream. While you can hold a vision for your future, give the universe some flexibility. Understand the universe knows what is best for you—and you don't.

Holding no specific agenda results in there being no separation between what *is* and what you desire. Being at peace with what is reinforces sustaining energy. When there is no discontinuity, there is no need for change, and your reality is sustained. If you are attached to a specific agenda, you will encounter suffering. Suffering energy invites in the forces of destruction that will work to end your suffering.

Making life a spiritual journey means you will be aware of the synchronicity that guides you. You will be grateful for the opportunities that show up, as if by magic. You will experience life as a magical journey.

Being Lost in the Moment

One day synchronicity will bring you to a moment where you know you're right where you're supposed to be, but you're lost. You don't know what to do next. You don't know which way to go. Then suddenly you notice something, and you know what you're going to do in the next moment. Saying this another way would describe how your soul's blueprint brought you to the point of being lost in a moment of time with no plan—a moment of pure *not-knowing*. This time, however, you're aware that you're standing in the center of the road written in your blueprint, but you can't see which way the blueprint wants you to go. Again, you're lost in the middle of nowhere.

The final scene in the movie *Castaway* depicts such a moment. Tom Hanks's character had delivered the FedEx box he held onto while he was lost on a small deserted island. His mission to deliver the box to its destination had been accomplished. He parked at a crossroads and contemplated what to do next. He had no plan. He didn't know what to do next. He was lost in the moment when a pickup truck came down the road. It stopped, and a nice woman told him where each road would take him. Then she drove away. As the Hanks's character watched her drive off, he *noticed* the wings painted on the tailgate of her truck. He knew where he was going next because they were the same wings that were painted on the FedEx box.

This is how you follow your blueprint. Notice what you notice and take action. When you don't know what to do, your life will unfold according to your blueprint, and you will fulfill your purpose.

The End

Printed in the United States
By Bookmasters